POWERPOINT 2000

in easy steps

Stephen Copestake

COMPUTER
STEP

In easy steps is an imprint of Computer Step
Southfield Road . Southam
Warwickshire CV33 OFB . England

Tel: 01926 817999 Fax: 01926 817005
http://www.computerstep.com

Notice of Liability

Every effort has been made to ensure that this book contains accurate
and current information. However, Computer Step and the author shall
not be liable for any loss or damage suffered by readers as a result of
any information contained herein.

Trademarks

Microsoft® and Windows® are registered trademarks of Microsoft
Corporation. All other trademarks are acknowledged as belonging to
their respective companies.

Printed and bound in the United Kingdom

ISBN 1-84078-043-6

Contents

6 Using multimedia   127

7 Finalising slide shows   145

First steps

This Chapter shows you how to launch PowerPoint 2000 and create new (or open existing) slide shows at the same time. You'll learn how to specify which toolbars display, how to work with differing document views and how to set Zoom levels. You'll also undo/redo errors; discover how to use PowerPoint 2000's inbuilt HELP system; and use Quick File Switching. Finally, you'll have PowerPoint find and repair basic program errors, and then close it down.

Covers

Chapter One

Starting PowerPoint 2000

Launching PowerPoint 2000 is a multi-stage process.

First, click this button on the Windows Task Bar at the base of the screen:

Now do the following:

Click here

You can create a shortcut to run PowerPoint 2000 directly. See your Windows documentation for how to do this.

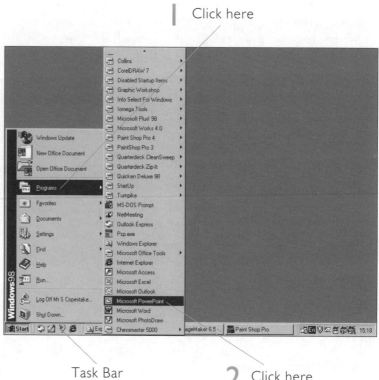

Task Bar

2 Click here

...cont'd

For more information on how to create new slide shows with:

- **the AutoContent Wizard**
- **templates**

see Chapter 2.

Before you carry out step 6, click Open an existing presentation.

Re steps 6-7 – as a shortcut, double-click a file here: to open a slide show directly.

PowerPoint 2000 now launches its Welcome screen. Do ONE of the following. Carry out step 3 below to create a new presentation with the AutoContent Wizard, or step 4 to create a new presentation based on a template. Alternatively, follow step 5 to create a blank slide show, or 6 to open one created earlier:

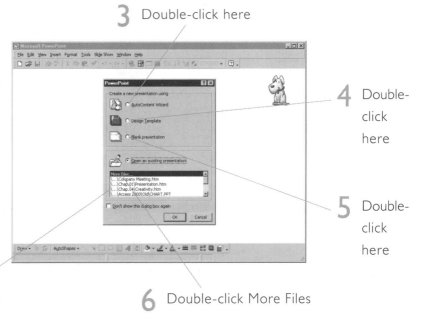

3 Double-click here

4 Double-click here

5 Double-click here

6 Double-click More Files

To locate the file you want to open, click here:
In the list, select the appropriate drive. Then double-click the relevant folder here:
Finally, carry out step 7.

If you carried out steps 3, 4 or 5, PowerPoint 2000 launches a variant of its main screen (see page 10 for more details). If, however, you followed step 6, the next dialog appears. Perform step 7 below:

Slide show preview

7 Double-click a slide show to open it

The PowerPoint 2000 screen

When you've instructed PowerPoint 2000 to create a new presentation based on a template or with the help of the AutoContent Wizard (see page 9), or if you've elected to open an existing presentation, the final result will look something like this:

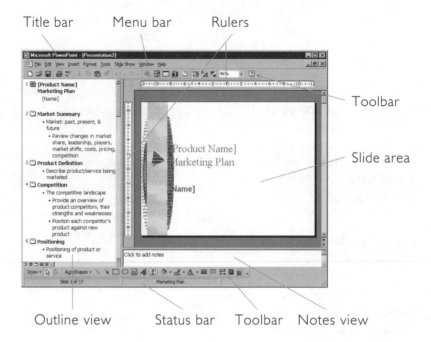

Title bar   Menu bar   Rulers

Toolbar

Slide area

Outline view   Status bar   Toolbar   Notes view

Note, however, that this is simply one 'view': Slide View. PowerPoint 2000 lets you interact with presentations in various ways. It does this by providing the following additional views:

*   Outline

*   Slide Sorter

*   Notes Page

See pages 18-19 later for more information.

Working with toolbars

Toolbars are collections of icons. By clicking on the appropriate icon, you can launch a specific PowerPoint 2000 feature. Using toolbars saves you having to pull down menus and use dialogs.

PowerPoint 2000 comes with 13 toolbars. Some of the most frequently used are:

Standard   The most useful toolbar. Use this to open and save presentations, and to perform copy/cut and paste operations. Also used to:

> — launch HELP
>
> — insert new slides
>
> — print presentations
>
> — change the slide Zoom level

Formatting   Use this to apply formatting options to slides and text

Drawing   Use this to create shapes and lines, and to customise shape and line colour/formatting

Picture   Use this to insert disk-based pictures into slides, and to format them

Web   Use this to go to World Wide Web sites instantly (providing you have a live Internet connection), and to navigate through Web pages once you've arrived

Clipboard   Use this to paste in multiple items from the PowerPoint 2000 Clipboard (see page 27)

Specifying which toolbars display

You can have as many toolbars on-screen as you need.

Pull down the View menu and carry out the following steps:

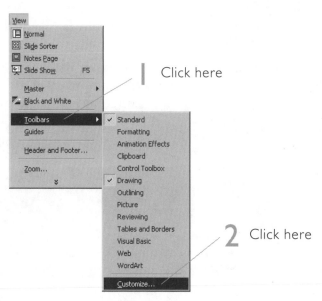

Click here

2 Click here

Re step 4 – to hide or reveal a toolbar, make sure you click the box to the left of the toolbar title:

(A tick in the box means the selected toolbar is currently on-screen.)

3 Ensure this tab is active

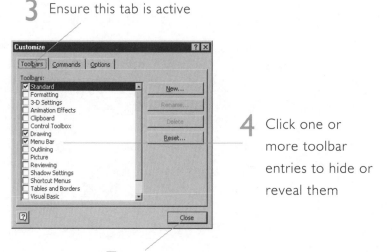

4 Click one or more toolbar entries to hide or reveal them

5 Click here

...cont'd

Adding new icons to toolbars

Ensure the toolbar you want to add a new feature icon to is currently on screen (if it isn't, follow steps 1-5 on page 12). Pull down the View menu and do the following:

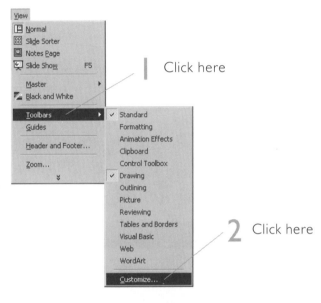

Click here

Re step 4 – toolbar commands are organised under overall categories (feature sets).

2 Click here

3 Ensure this tab is active

To *delete* an existing toolbar icon, follow steps 1-3. Then drag the icon off the toolbar. (When you release the mouse button, it disappears.) Finally, carry out step 6.

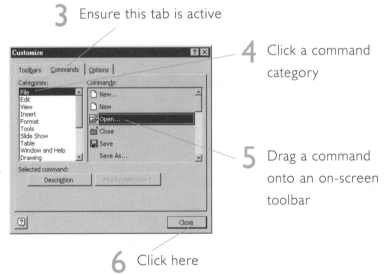

4 Click a command category

5 Drag a command onto an on-screen toolbar

6 Click here

Automatic customisation

A long-standing anomaly in the use of software has been that, although different users use different features, no allowance has been made for this: the same features display on everyone's menus and toolbars...

Now this has changed. In PowerPoint 2000, menus and toolbars are personalised.

Personalised menus

When you first use PowerPoint 2000, its menus display the features which Microsoft believes are used 95% of the time. Features which are infrequently used are not immediately visible. This is made clear in the illustrations below:

Menus expand of their own accord, after a time. However, to expand them manually, click the chevrons:

The Format menu, as it first appears...

As you use menus, individual features are dynamically promoted or demoted, as appropriate.
  This means menus are continually evolving. It also means that the menus shown in this book may not correspond exactly to those you see on your screen...

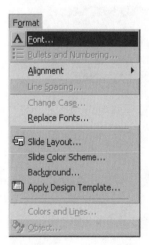

The expanded menu – the little-used features are shown in paler grey

Personalised toolbars

Toolbars in PowerPoint 2000 work on a similar principle to menus:

- if possible, they display on a single row

- they overlap when there isn't enough room on-screen

- icons are 'promoted' and 'demoted' like menu entries

Look at the illustration below:

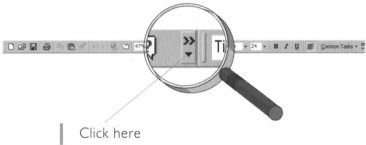

Click here

 You can use this fly-out as an alternative way to add new buttons to toolbars.
Place the mouse pointer over Add or Remove Buttons. In the menu which appears, do one of the following:

- **click an entry which doesn't have ☑ against it to add it to the main toolbar**

- **click an entry which does have ☑ against it to remove it from the main toolbar**

Here, two toolbars (Standard on the left and Formatting on the right) are displaying side by side. As a result, not all of the buttons display. Following step 1 above produces this result:

Icons PowerPoint has determined are little used display in a separate fly-out

To implement any of the hidden features, simply click the relevant icon.

Undo and Redo

You can even undo an undo. In PowerPoint 2000, this is called 'redoing' – see 'Redoing an action' below.

A very useful feature in PowerPoint 2000 is the ability to undo – or reverse – editing actions. Most editing actions can be undone with a couple of mouse clicks or a keyboard command. The main exceptions are:

- changing Zoom levels

- opening or saving files

PowerPoint 2000 even lets you specify the number of consecutive undos.

Re step 2 in both undoing and redoing – selecting an action which isn't at the top of the list affects earlier actions, too.

Undoing an action
In the Standard toolbar, do the following:

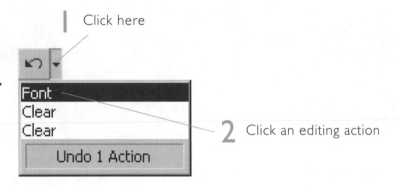

Click here

2 Click an editing action

You can use the following keyboard shortcuts:

Ctrl+Z   Undo
Ctrl+Y   Redo
to undo/redo *single* actions.

Redoing an action
In the Standard toolbar, do the following:

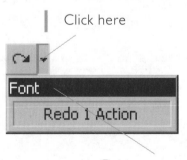

Click here

2 Click an editing action

If you haven't used the Redo button before, it may be on the Standard toolbar fly-out rather than the toolbar itself.

...cont'd

You can determine how many Undo levels PowerPoint 2000 supports.

Setting Undo levels

Pull down the Tools menu and do the following:

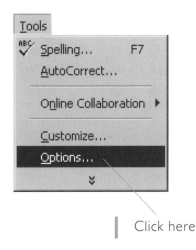

Click here

2 Ensure this tab is active

Re step 3 – the default number of undos is 20.

The maximum number is 150.

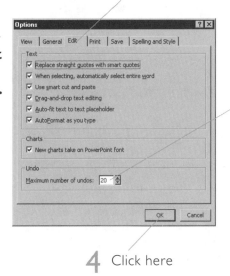

3 Type in the number of undos you need

4 Click here

The slide views – an overview

Normal view also includes the following:

- **Outline view – shows the textual structure underlying slides**
- **Notes view – shows the speaker notes associated with the active slide**

There are also various Master views – see chapter 3 for how to use these.

These views are discussed in greater detail in later chapters.

PowerPoint has the following views:

Normal   displays each slide individually

Slide Sorter   shows all the slides as icons, so you can manipulate them more easily

Notes Page   shows each slide together with any speaker notes

These are different ways of looking at your slide show. Normal view provides a very useful overview, while Slide Sorter view lets you modify more than one slide at a time.

Switching to a view

Pull down the View menu and click Normal, Slide Sorter or Notes Page.

The three views are compared below:

Normal view

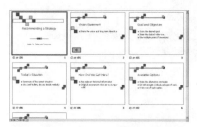

Slide Sorter view

Notes Page view

Using the slide views

The following are some brief supplemental notes on how best to use the PowerPoint 2000 views.

Normal view

Normal view displays the current slide in its own window. Use Normal view when you want a detailed picture of a slide (for instance, when you amend any of the slide contents, or when you change the overall formatting).

You can also use Normal view to:

In Normal and Notes Page views, you can also use the vertical scroll bar to move to specific slides.

As you drag the scroll bar, PowerPoint 2000 displays a message telling you the number and title of the slide you're up to:

Slide: 1 of 2
[Company Name] Certificat...

- work with text. The Outline view component – see page 8 – displays only text. You can amend this and watch your changes take effect in the Slide area on the right

- enter notes. Simply click in the Notes view below the Slide area and enter speaker note text. (You can also do this within Notes Page view – see below)

To switch from slide to slide, you can press Page Up or Page Down as appropriate.

Slide Sorter view

If you need to rearrange the order of slides, use Slide Sorter view. You can simply click on a slide and drag it to a new location (to move more than one slide, hold down one Ctrl key as you click them, then release the key and drag). You can also copy a slide by holding down Ctrl *as you drag*.

You can also use Slide Sorter view to perform additional operations – for instance, you can use it to apply a new slide layout to more than one slide at a time. (See chapter 2 for how to do this.)

Notes Page view

This view is an aid to the presenter rather than the viewer of the slide show. If you want to enter speaker notes on a slide (for later printing), use Notes Page view.

In Notes Page view, the slide is displayed at a reduced size at the top of the page. Below this is a PowerPoint 2000 text object. For how to enter notes in this, see page 44.

Using Zoom

You can also use the Zoom button to set Zoom levels.
In the Standard toolbar, do the following:

It's often useful to be able to inspect your presentations in close up; this is called 'zooming in'. Alternatively, sometimes taking an overview ('zooming out') is beneficial.

You can zoom in and out in any PowerPoint 2000 view (although the available options vary).

Click the arrow, then select a level

Setting the Zoom level

Pull down the View menu and do the following:

Re the above tip – if you haven't used it before, the Zoom button may be on the Standard toolbar fly-out instead.

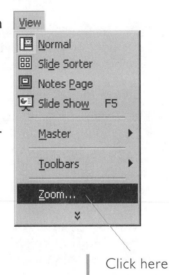

Click here

If you want to use your own Zoom level (rather than a set figure), type in the zoom % here:
Finally, carry out step 3.

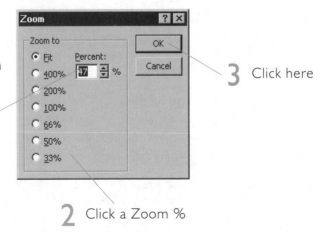

3 Click here

2 Click a Zoom %

Using HELP

Office supports the standard Windows HELP system. For instance:

These highly specific HELP bubbles are called 'ToolTips'. ToolTips are a specialised form of ScreenTips (see below).

- Moving the mouse pointer over toolbar buttons produces an explanatory HELP bubble:

To close any HELP window, simply press Esc.

- You can move the mouse pointer over fields in dialogs, commands or screen areas and produce a specific HELP box. Carry out the following procedure to achieve this:

Right-clicking a field and left-clicking the box which launches...

These highly specific HELP topics are called 'ScreenTips'.

Displays Help text, explaining what the command does.

...produces a specific HELP topic

Other standard Windows HELP features are also present; see your Windows documentation for how to use these. Additionally, PowerPoint 2000 has inbuilt HELP in the normal way...

(PowerPoint also has one unique HELP feature: the Office Assistant. See the next topic.)

Using the Office Assistant

The Office Assistant is animated. It can also change shape! To do this, click the Options button. In the dialog which appears, activate the Gallery tab. Click the Next button until the Assistant you want is displayed. Click OK, then follow any further on-screen instructions.

PowerPoint 2000 has a unique HELP feature which is designed to make it much easier to become productive: the Office Assistant. The Assistant:

- answers questions directly. This is an especially useful feature for the reason that, normally when you invoke a program's HELP system, you know more or less the question you want to ask, or the topic on which you need information. If neither of these is true, however, the Office Assistant responds to plain English questions and provides a choice of answers. For example, responses produced by entering 'What are ToolTips?' include:

  — *Show or hide shortcut keys in ScreenTips*

  — *Show or hide toolbar ScreenTips*

  — *Rename a menu command or toolbar button*

- provides context-sensitive tips

- answers questions in your own words

The Office Assistant also provides specific help for known problem areas – see page 25.

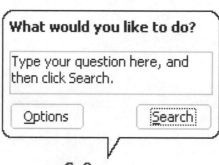

The Office Assistant, after it has just launched

If the HELP bubble isn't displayed, simply click anywhere in the Assistant:

...cont'd

You can also use a keyboard shortcut to launch the Office Assistant. Simply press F1.

Launching the Office Assistant

By default, the Office Assistant displays automatically. If it isn't currently on-screen, however, refer to the Standard toolbar and do the following:

Click here

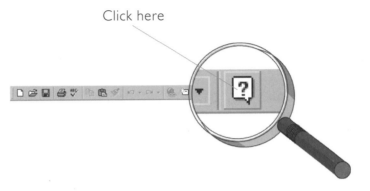

To close an Office Assistant window at any time, press Esc, or click the Close button.

Hiding the Office Assistant

If you don't want the Office Assistant to display, right-click over it and do the following:

If you don't want to use the Office Assistant at all, do the following.
  Click here:
In the Office Assistant dialog, activate the Options tab. Deselect Use the Office Assistant. Click OK.

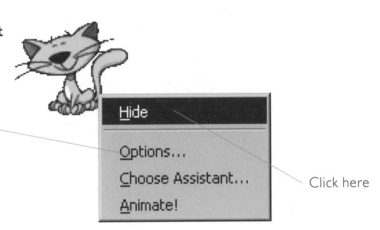

Click here

...cont'd

If the Assistant doesn't provide the right answer, you can send your query to a special Web site with more information.

Ensure your Internet connection is live, then do the following:

Click here

Now click:

Send and go to the Web

in the HELP window which launches. In the Office update Web site do ONE of the following:

• **click an article link e.g.**

Animated Templates for PowerPoint

• **click this button to search for further help:**

Search

You can use the Office Assistant (whatever its current incarnation) to ask questions in plain English. The advantage of using the Assistant to do this is that you can use it to find information on topics which you aren't sure how to classify.

Asking questions

First, ensure the Office Assistant is visible. Carry out steps 1-2, then perform step 3 OR 4:

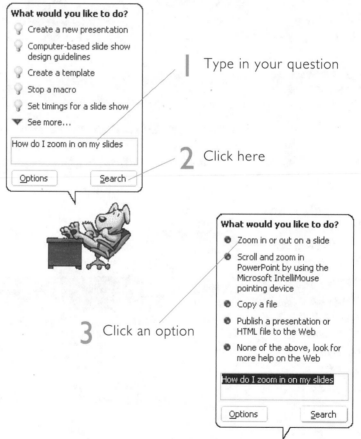

1 Type in your question

2 Click here

3 Click an option

4 If available, click: ▼ **See more...** In the list of further topics, click one; or (if none of them are germane) follow the procedures in the tip

The Presentation Assistant

The Presentation Assistant is the name Microsoft gives to a special PowerPoint implementation of the Office Assistant.

Prolonged user studies have shown that there are aspects to using PowerPoint 2000 which give rise to particular difficulty. As a result, the Office Assistant has been extended to provide special help with these. Look at the example below:

Double-clicking this picture (in an attempt to edit it) has produced the message on the left

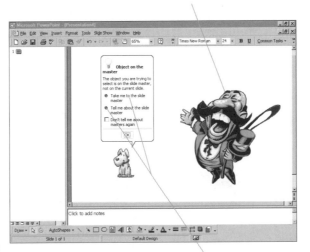

This is an active slide...

Click an option

Because the picture is on the Master, it appears on every slide in the host presentation but can only be edited within the Master. (For more information on slide masters, see chapter 3.)

The attempt to edit the picture has failed because – despite appearances – the clip art original is on the Slide Master, not the active slide. As a result, the Presentation Assistant has:

1. detected the editing attempt

2. recognised it as a difficult area

3. launched a message with the solution (in this case, carry out step 1)

Install on Demand

After step 2, the missing component is installed. In this case, Organization Chart launches with a sample org chart:

Toolbar

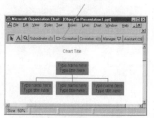

Do the following, as appropriate:

- **click in the title and amend this**
- **click in one or more boxes and amend the text**
- **to add a new box, click the relevant option in the Toolbar, then move the mouse pointer over a box and left-click once**
- **when you've finished, pull down the File menu and click Update... (the ellipses denote your slide show). Now press Alt+F4**

PowerPoint 2000 makes use of a new feature which allows users to install program components on demand, only when they're needed. Uninstalled components still have the following triggers:

- shortcuts

- icons

- menu entries

within PowerPoint 2000.

An example of Install on Demand is Organization Chart (a special program component used to create org charts). Following step 1 to insert an org chart into a slide:

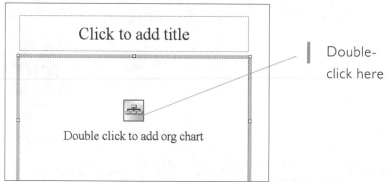

Double-click here

produces (since Organization Chart is not installed by default) a special message. Do the following:

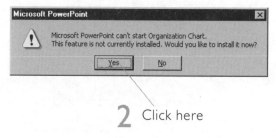

2 Click here

Collect and Paste

In earlier versions of PowerPoint, if you wanted to copy-and-paste multiple items of text and/or pictures into a presentation, it was necessary (since the Windows Clipboard can only hold one item at a time) to perform each operation separately. Now, however, you can use the new Collect and Paste operation to make this much easier.

Using Collect and Paste

Collect and Paste uses a special Clipboard which is exclusive to PowerPoint 2000. Up to 12 items can be stored in it at the same time.

Use standard procedures to copy multiple examples of text and/or pictures – after the first copy, the Clipboard Toolbar launches. Now do the following:

1 (If appropriate) click where you want to paste in an item

The Clipboard Toolbar – the icons on the right denote copied text, those on the left copied pictures

To clear the contents of the PowerPoint 2000 Clipboard, click this button:

in the toolbar.

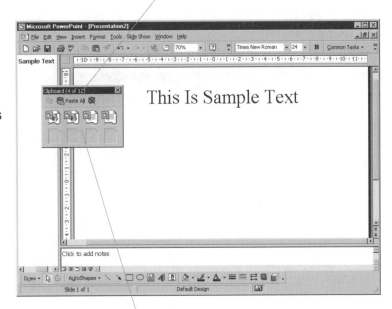

2 Click an icon to paste in the contents

Quick File Switching

In the past, only programs (not individual windows within programs) displayed on the Windows Taskbar. With PowerPoint 2000, however, all open windows display as separate buttons.

In the following example, three new slide shows have been created. All three display as separate windows, although only one copy of PowerPoint 2000 is running:

To use
**Quick File
Switching
you need:**

- **Windows 98/ 2000, or;**
- **Windows 95 with Internet Explorer 4.0 (or higher)**

The Windows Taskbar

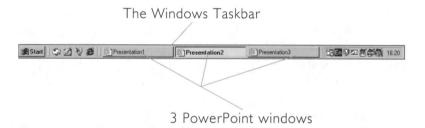

3 PowerPoint windows

This is clarified by a glance at PowerPoint 2000's Window menu which shows all open windows:

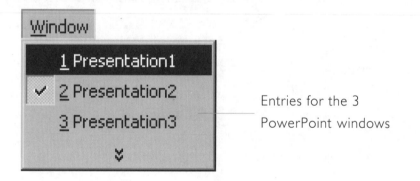

Entries for the 3 PowerPoint windows

Use this technique to go to a presentation by simply clicking its Taskbar button, a considerable saving in time and effort.

Repairing errors

PowerPoint 2000 provides the following:

Automatic repair

Whenever you start PowerPoint 2000, it:

1. determines if essential files are missing or corrupted

2. automatically reinstalls the files, if necessary

3. repairs incorrect entries (relating to missing or corrupted files) in the Windows Registry

Manual repair

There are other potential problems which, though far less serious, can still result in lost productivity – e.g. corrupted fonts and missing templates.

PowerPoint 2000 has a special diagnostic procedure (called 'Detect and Repair') which you can run when necessary. The procedure:

1. scrutinises the original state of your installation

2. compares this with the present state of your installation

3. takes the appropriate remedial steps

To run Detect and Repair, pull down the Help menu and do the following:

 The Detect and Repair process is often lengthy.

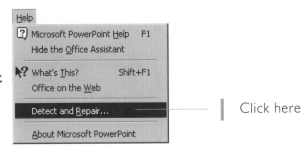

Click here

2 In the Detect and Repair message, click: Start

PowerPoint 2000 now detects and remedies any problem – follow the on-screen instructions.

Closing down PowerPoint 2000

To close down PowerPoint 2000 when you've finished using it, pull down the File menu and do the following:

Click here

If there are any unsaved changes to current presentations, PowerPoint 2000 now produces a special message.

Carry out step 1 below to save your work and then close PowerPoint 2000. Alternatively, follow step 2 to close PowerPoint 2000 *without* saving your work:

2 Click here

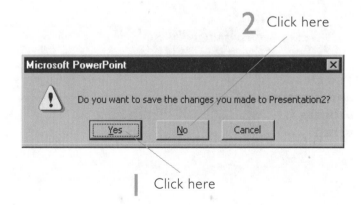

Click here

Creating a slide show

Use this chapter to acquire the basics of producing your own slide show. You'll also learn how to apply new layouts to slides, and how to use existing text placeholders as a shortcut to text entry. Additionally, you'll have text errors corrected automatically; create your own text boxes; format inserted text (including applying bullets); search for and replace text; and then spell-check it. You'll go on to work with slide outlines and save your work to disk. Finally, you'll also discover how to save your slide shows to the Internet/intranets.

Covers

Chapter Two

Creating slide shows – an overview

PowerPoint 2000 lets you create a new presentation in the following ways (in descending order of ease of use):

- with the help of the AutoContent Wizard

- by basing it on a template, and creating each slide and its contents (apart from the background) manually

- by creating a blank presentation, and creating each slide and its contents (including the background) manually

 When you create slide shows based on templates, you can use a shortcut. If applicable, you can simply edit the text placeholders inserted when you apply AutoLayouts (pre-defined formatting schemes), rather than create your own text boxes.

(See page 44 for how to edit existing placeholders, or page 48 for how to add and complete your own text boxes.)

The AutoContent Wizard is a high-powered yet easy to use shortcut to creating a slide show. It incorporates a question-and-answer system. You work through a series of dialogs, answering the appropriate questions and making the relevant choices. This is the easiest way to produce a slide show, but the results are nonetheless highly professional.

Templates – also known as boilerplates – are sample presentations, complete with the relevant formatting and/or text. By basing a new slide show on a template, you automatically have access to these. Templates don't offer as many formatting choices as the AutoContent Wizard, but the results are equally as professional.

Slide shows created with the use of templates or the AutoContent Wizard can easily be amended subsequently.

Creating blank presentations is the simplest route; use this if you want to define the slide show components yourself from scratch. This is often not the most efficient or effective way to create new presentations. However, it isn't as onerous as might be imagined because PowerPoint 2000 lets you apply the following:

- pre-defined slide layouts (to individual slides) – see the tip

- slide designs based on templates (see Chapter 3)

Using the AutoContent Wizard

When you use the AutoContent wizard, you create a presentation which contains pre-defined content and design elements (although you can easily change as many of these as you want later). You can also choose from a large number of presentation types; these are organised under several headings (e.g. General, Corporate and Projects) and are suitable for most purposes.

 You also have the chance to launch the AutoContent Wizard as soon as you start PowerPoint 2000. Follow step 3 on page 9, then carry out steps 4-12 on pages 34-36.

Launching the AutoContent Wizard

Pull down the File menu and carry out the following steps:

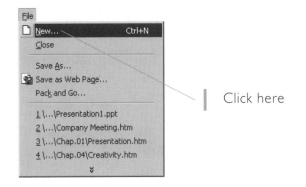

Click here

2 Ensure this tab is active

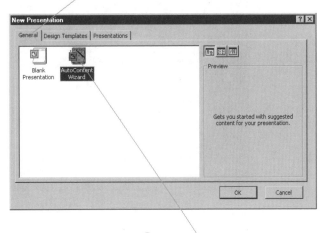

3 Double-click here

Now carry out the following steps:

If the Office Assistant is on-screen, it provides specific help with using the AutoContent Wizard:

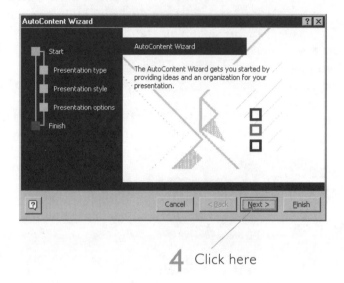

4 Click here

5 Click a slide show heading

6 Click a slide show type

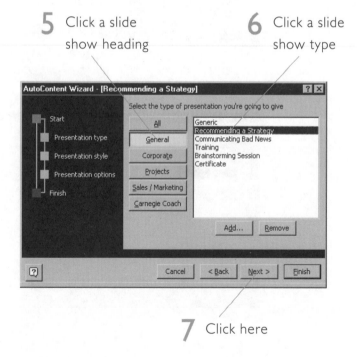

7 Click here

Carry out the following additional steps:

**Re step 8 –
To have
PowerPoint
2000
apply a colour
scheme which is
suitable for use on
the Internet or
intranets, select
Web presentation.
(For more on
colour schemes, see
Chapter 3.)**

8 Select an output type

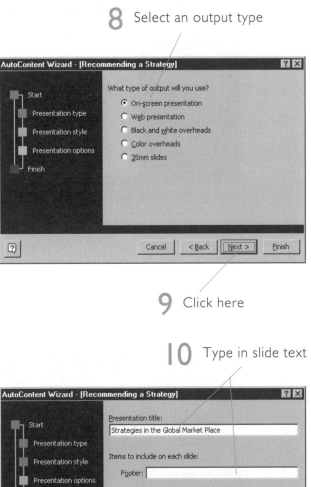

9 Click here

10 Type in slide text

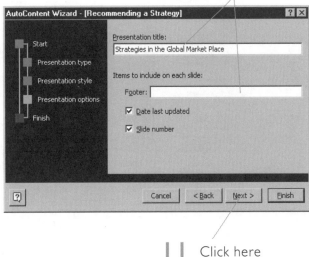

11 Click here

Now carry out the following step:

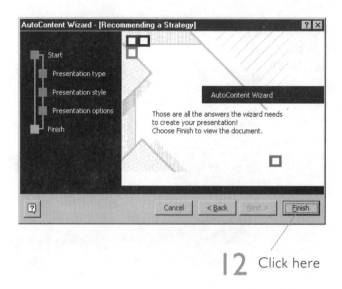

12 Click here

PowerPoint 2000 creates the new presentation:

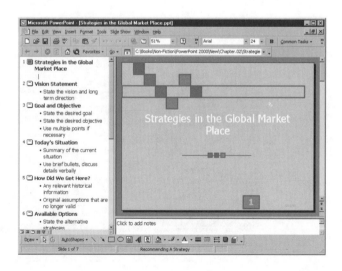

The final
slide show,
in Normal
view

Using templates

With some layouts, you can also add:

- **pictures/clip art (see chapter 6)**
- **org charts (see chapter 1), and/or;**
- **charts (see chapter 5)**

You also have the chance to create a new slide show based on a template as soon as you start PowerPoint 2000. Follow step 4 on page 9. Then carry out steps 3-4 on page 38. (Also, perform the procedures on page 39 as often as necessary, to create additional slides.)

When you create a slide show with the help of a template, you:

1. select a template
2. apply a pre-defined layout
3. type in the textual content (but see the DON'T FORGET tip)

Step 1 applies to the overall presentation, while steps 2 and 3 have to be undertaken for every individual slide. This makes creating new presentations based on templates a rather longer process than using the AutoContent Wizard. However, the end result is likely to be more personalised, and it is easier to have variations in individual style layout, if you need this.

Creating a new slide show based on a template

Pull down the File menu and do the following:

Click here

...cont'd

You can use the dialog shown on the right to create a new slide show optimised for use on intranets.

Follow step 1 on page 37. In step 2, activate the Presentations tab (then ignore the remaining steps on this and the facing page). Double-click this icon:

Group Home Page

This is the result:

Now carry out the following additional steps:

2 Ensure this tab is active

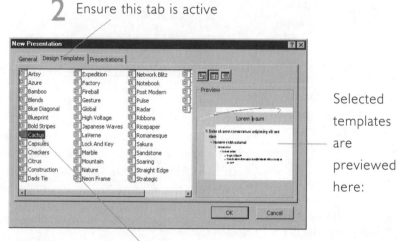

Selected templates are previewed here:

3 Double-click a template

4 Double-click a layout

PowerPoint 2000 now creates the Title slide (slide number 1) for your presentation.

...cont'd

The Title slide for the new presentation is shown below:

 This is a picture placeholder – see chapter 6 for how to use it:

Text placeholders

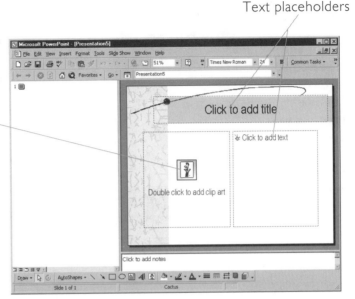

5 Click in the text placeholders and type in the necessary text (for more information on how to do this, see page 44).

Creating additional slides

When you've finished filling in the Title slide, pull down the Insert menu and do the following to create a new slide based on the template you selected in step 3 on page 38:

 After step 1, follow step 4 on page 38 to assign a slide layout.

Repeat the procedures described under 'Creating additional slides' for as many new slides as you want to insert.

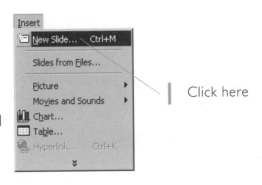

Click here

Creating blank slide shows

To create a blank slide show, pull down the File menu and do the following:

You also have the chance to create a new blank slide show as soon as you start PowerPoint 2000.

Follow step 5 on page 9. Then carry out steps 4-5 on page 41.

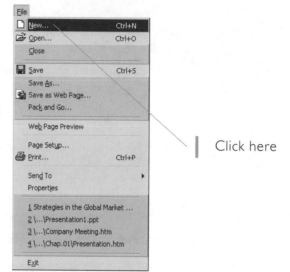

Click here

2 Ensure this tab is active

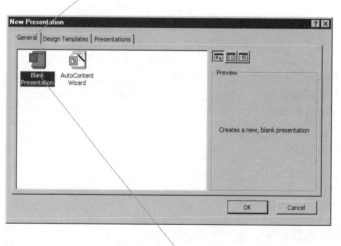

3 Double-click here

...cont'd

Carry out the following additional step:

4 Double-click a layout

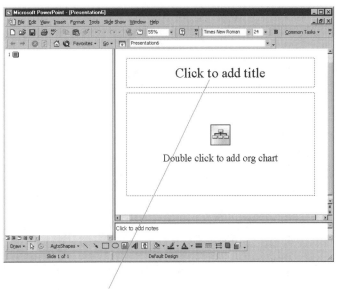

The resulting Title slide for a new blank presentation is shown below:

When you've finished filling in the Title slide, follow the procedures under 'Creating additional slides' on page 39 to:

- **add new slides**
- **assign layouts to them, and;**
- **insert text in the relevant placeholders**

Text placeholder

5 Click in the text placeholders and type in the necessary text (for more information on how to do this, see page 44).

Customising slide structure

Once you've created a slide show (using any of the methods discussed earlier), the easiest way to customise the basic format of a slide is to use AutoLayout. AutoLayout offers a selection of 24 layout structures and lets you apply your choice to a specific slide or group of slides. You can then amend the individual components (see later topics).

You can select more than one slide in Slide Sorter view by holding down Shift as you click on the slide icons.

Using AutoLayout

Make sure you're in Normal or Slide Sorter view (see page 18 for how to switch between views). If you're in Slide Sorter view, select the slide(s) you want to amend. Pull down the Format menu and do the following:

You can also customise slide shows by applying design templates – see Chapter 3.

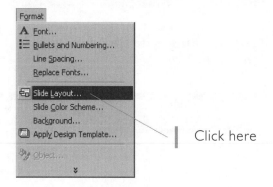

Click here

2 Click a slide format

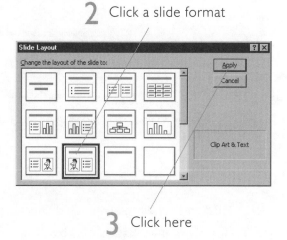

3 Click here

Any slide components present before you applied the new format will still remain. However, they may need to be resized or moved. Look at the illustrations below:

Before...

Text object

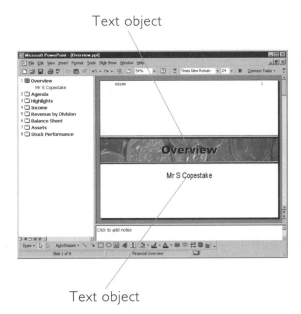

The original slide...

Text object

After...

Use standard mouse techniques to reposition or rescale text objects in PowerPoint 2000.

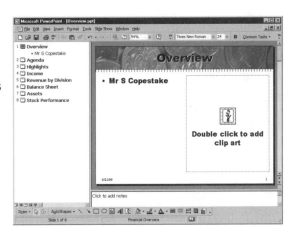

... and after a new layout has been applied – the text objects have been moved

Adding text to slides

When you create a new slide show (with one exception – see the tip), PowerPoint 2000 fills each slide with placeholders containing sample text. The idea is that you should replace this with your own text.

The illustration below shows a sample slide before customisation:

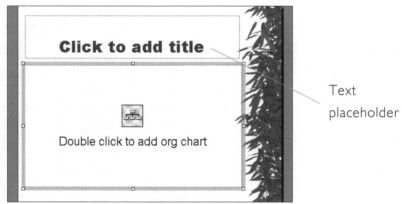

Text placeholder

To insert your own text, click in any text placeholder. PowerPoint displays a text entry box. Do the following:

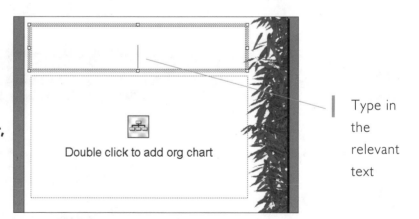

Type in the relevant text

2 Finally, click anywhere outside the placeholder to confirm the addition of the new text.

AutoCorrect – an overview

AutoCorrect is a very useful PowerPoint 2000 feature. Its principal purpose is to correct typing errors automatically. It does this by maintaining a list of inaccurate spellings and their corrected versions. When you press the Spacebar or Enter/Return keys immediately after making a mistake, the correction is substituted for the original error.

AutoCorrect is supplied with a long list of preset corrections. The following are examples:

- allwasy **becomes** always

- acomodate **becomes** accommodate

- alot **becomes** a lot

- do'nt **becomes** don't

- garantee **becomes** guarantee

- oppertunity **becomes** opportunity

- wierd **becomes** weird

In addition, however, you can easily define your own. If, for instance, you regularly type lthe when you mean the, you can have AutoCorrect make the correction for you.

You can also enter shortened forms of correct words – or entire phrases – and have them expanded automatically. (For instance, you could have AutoCorrect expand ann into Annual Profit Forecast...)

AutoCorrect has further uses. You can have:

1. the first letters of sentences capitalised

2. words which begin with two capitals corrected (e.g. 'HEllo' becomes 'Hello')

3. days capitalised (e.g. 'monday' becomes 'Monday')

Customising AutoCorrect

You can add new corrections, delete existing ones or specify which AutoCorrect functions are active.

Adding new corrections
Pull down the Tools menu and do the following:

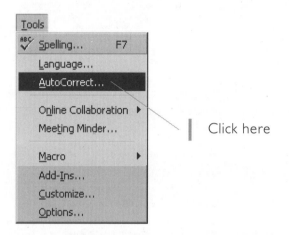

Click here

If you don't want errors corrected automatically, deselect Replace text as you type.

2 Type in the incorrect word

3 Type in the correction

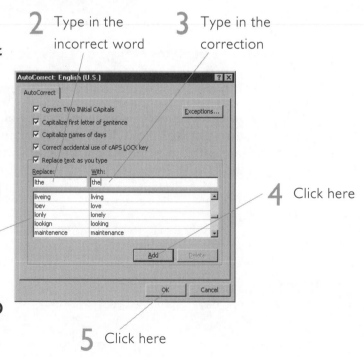

4 Click here

To remove an entry, select it here:

Click this button:

PowerPoint 2000 deletes the item immediately.

5 Click here

...cont'd

Setting other AutoCorrect options

Perform step 1 on page 46. Now do the following:

An exception is a letter or word (followed by a full stop) after which you don't want the first letter of the following word capitalised.

Ensure the First Letter tab is active before you carry out steps A–C.

This dialog does not distinguish between lower- and upper-case.
For example, entering:
quart.
has the same effect as entering:
Quart.

After step C, carry out step 3 above.

2 Deselect any of these options

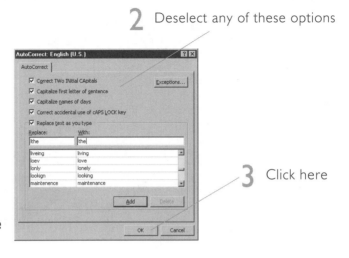

3 Click here

Specifying exceptions

There are situations where PowerPoint's automatic capitalisation is wrong. For instance, if you type in approx. followed by another word, the first letter of the second word is capitalised due to the preceding full stop, which may not be what you want. To prevent this happening, you can set up an exception.

In the above dialog, click this button – Exceptions... – and do the following:

A Type in an exception

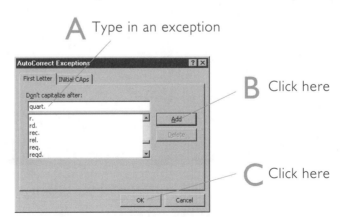

B Click here

C Click here

Inserting text boxes

If a slide contains no text placeholders, you can still insert text easily and conveniently by creating and inserting a text box.

Creating a text box

Refer to the Drawing toolbar. (If it isn't on-screen, pull down the View menu and click Toolbars, Drawing.) Do the following:

 This way of defining a text box ensures that the text you enter subsequently is subject to wrap (i.e. surplus text automatically moves to the next line).

If you don't want this, follow step 1. Omit steps 2-3. Then click where you want the text to appear and begin typing immediately. PowerPoint 2000 extends the containing text box to ensure that the text stays on the original line.

Click here

2 Move the mouse cursor over the slide and position it where you want the text box to begin. Drag to define the text box. Release the mouse button

3 Type in the relevant text. Press Enter when you've finished

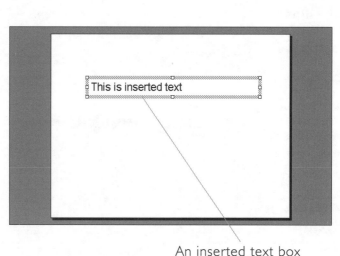

An inserted text box

Formatting text

You can carry out a variety of formatting enhancements on text. You can:

- change the font and/or type size

- apply a font style or effect

- apply a colour

- specify the alignment and/or line spacing

- insert tabs/indents

- apply/modify bullets

Re step 4 – styles you can apply are:

- **Bold**
- **Italic, and;**
- **Bold/Italic**

(Depending on the font selected in step 1, not all of them may be available.)

Font-based formatting

Click inside the relevant text object then select the text you want to format. Pull down the Format menu and click Font. Carry out any of steps 1-6 below, as appropriate. Then follow step 7:

Re step 6 – if none of the colours here are suitable, click More Colors. In the new dialog, click a colour in the polygon in the centre. Then click OK. Finally, follow step 7.

1 Click a new typeface

2 Type in a new point size

7 Click here

5 Click here

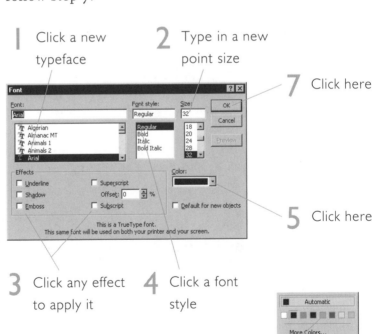

3 Click any effect to apply it

4 Click a font style

6 Click a colour (see the HOT TIP)

Some examples of line spacing in action:

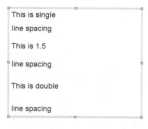

Changing text spacing

First, click inside the relevant text object and select the text whose spacing you want to amend. Pull down the Format menu and click Line Spacing. Now carry out any of steps 1-3 below, as appropriate. Then follow step 4.

Type in a line spacing

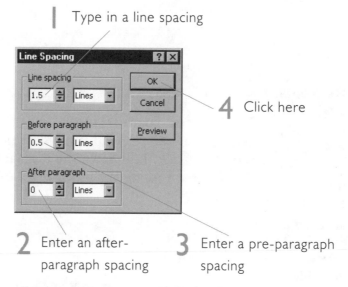

4 Click here

2 Enter an after-paragraph spacing

3 Enter a pre-paragraph spacing

Some examples of alignment in action:

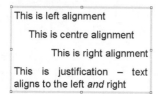

Changing text alignment

First, click inside the relevant text object and select the text whose alignment you want to amend. Pull down the Format menu and do the following:

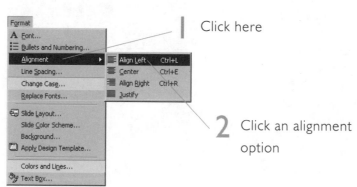

Click here

2 Click an alignment option

...cont'd

If the ruler isn't currently visible, pull down the View menu and click Ruler.

To delete a tab stop, simply drag it off the ruler.

Never use the Space bar to indent text: spaces vary in size according to the typeface and type size applying, and therefore give uneven results.

Re step 2 in 'Applying indents' – drag the square component:
 Here to revise the indent for *all* lines equally.

Applying tabs

First, click inside the relevant text object. Ensure the ruler is on-screen. Now do the following:

Click where you want the tab stop to appear

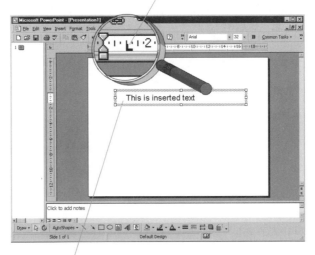

Here, step 2 has forced the text to the right

2 Back in the text, click where you want the tab to take effect and press the Tab key

Applying indents

First, click inside the relevant text object. Ensure the ruler is on-screen. Now do the following, as appropriate:

Drag this to revise the first-line indent

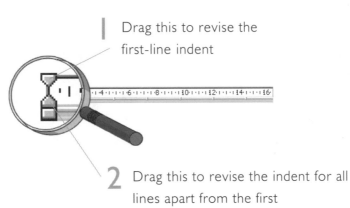

2 Drag this to revise the indent for all lines apart from the first

Bulleting text

Text in slides is often bulleted, for increased impact:

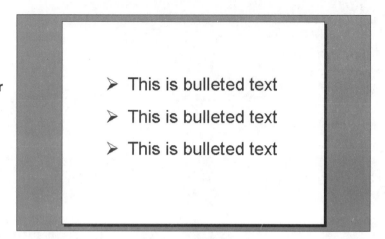

To add bullets to text, do the following:

1 Click in the relevant text block and select the text you want to reformat

2 Pull down the Format menu and click Bullets and Numbering

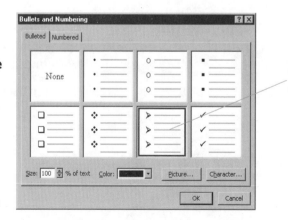

3 Double-click a bullet

Working with slide outlines

You can use the Outline component of Normal view (called Outline view) to organize and develop the content of your presentation.

In Outline view, you can:

You can have PowerPoint 2000 collect titles on specified slides and insert them into a new slide.

In Outline view, select the relevant slides by holding down Shift as you click:

in the Outline tree. Then click the Summary Slide button:

in the Outlining toolbar. PowerPoint inserts the new slide in front of the 1st selected slide.

- build presentation structures

- move entire slides from one position to another

- edit text entries

- hide or display text levels

Creating a presentation structure

First create a presentation, using any of the methods discussed earlier in this chapter. If necessary, pull down the View menu and click Normal. Now carry out step 1 below:

Click a slide entry

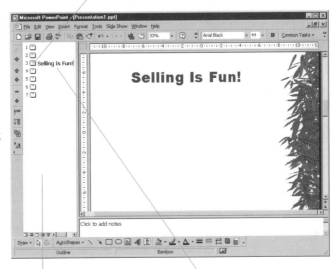

Outline view

2 Type in title text and press Enter (the change is reflected in the slide itself)

...cont'd

Now refer to the Outlining toolbar and do the following:

If the Outlining toolbar isn't on-screen, pull down the View menu and click Toolbars, Outlining.

3 Click here

'Demoting' a text entry moves it to a lower level.

When you press Enter in step 2 on page 53, PowerPoint 2000 creates a second title entry. Step 3 'demotes' it to a bulleted entry. Do the following:

4 Type in sub-text and press Enter

If you need to 'promote' a text entry (i.e. move it to a higher level), click in it. Then click this button in the Outlining toolbar:

To demote a text entry manually, click in it. Then click this button in the Outlining toolbar:

Repeat step 4 above as often as necessary. Finally, when you've finished creating text entries for the title slide, press Ctrl+Enter. This takes you to the next slide; use the techniques we've just discussed to add text to this. Repeat these procedures for as many slides as you want to include.

...cont'd

Re step 1 – to select multiple slides in Outline view, hold down one Shift key as you click their markers.

You can also move demoted entries *within* slides.

Ignore step 1. Double-click a demoted entry e.g.

• So sell as much as you can!

In step 2, move the entry to a new level within the original slide.

You can combine both procedures described here.

For instance, if you drag a demoted entry to a new blank slide, PowerPoint promotes it to a title...

Moving slides

To reposition slides in Outline view, carry out the following steps:

1 Click a slide marker

```
1 ☐ Selling is Fun!
        • So sell as much as you
          can!
        • To as many people as you
          can!
2 ☐
3 ☐
4 ☐
5 ☐
```

2 Drag the slide to a new location in the Outline tree

The end result:

```
1 ☐
2 ☐ Selling is Fun!
        • So sell as much as you
          can!
        • To as many people as you
          can!
3 ☐
4 ☐
5 ☐
```

What was previously slide 1 is now slide 2...

Hiding/displaying entries

An important feature of PowerPoint 2000's Outline view is the ability to hide or reveal entries at will. This enables you to alternate between achieving a useful overview and viewing entries in detail. Do the following:

Click in the outline entry you want to hide or expand

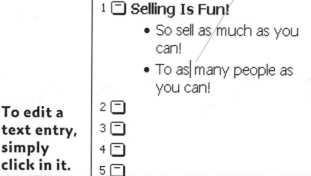

 To edit a text entry, simply click in it. Then use standard Windows text editing techniques. Click outside the entry when you've finished.

2 In the Outlining toolbar, click ▬ to hide the entry OR ✚ to expand it

The end result:

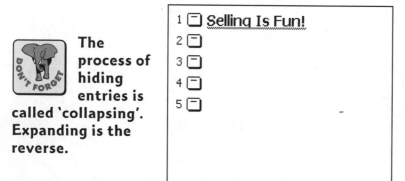

The process of hiding entries is called 'collapsing'. Expanding is the reverse.

The bulleted entries in the example above have now been (temporarily) hidden

Searching for text

PowerPoint 2000 lets you search for specific text within a slide show. For example, you can if you want have PowerPoint 2000 locate (successively) all instances of the word 'Money'.

You can also:

• limit the search to words which match the case of the text you specify (e.g. if you search for 'Money', PowerPoint 2000 will not go to slides which contain 'money' or 'MONEY')

• limit the search to whole words (e.g. if you search for 'pound', PowerPoint 2000 will not find slides which contain 'pounds')

Initiating a text search

Pull down the Edit menu and click Find. Now do the following:

You can use the Find dialog to replace text.

Click this button:

Now follow steps 1-5 as appropriate on page 58.

1   Type in the text you want to find

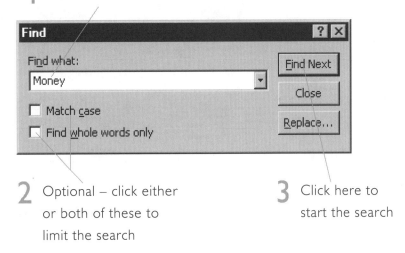

2   Optional – click either or both of these to limit the search

3   Click here to start the search

Step 3 locates the first instance of the search text; repeat it to locate the next. And so on...

Replacing text

When you've located text, you can have PowerPoint 2000 replace it automatically (or one instance at a time) with the text of your choice.

When you undertake a find-and-replace operation, you can (as with find operations) make the search component case-specific, or limit it to whole-word matches. (See page 57 for illustrations of both of these restrictions.)

Initiating a find-and-replace operation

First pull down the Edit menu and click Replace. Now follow steps 1 and 2 below. Carry out step 3, if appropriate. Finally, follow either step 4 OR 5:

1 Type in the text you want to find

2 Type in the replacement text

4 Click here to replace the 1st instance of the specified text

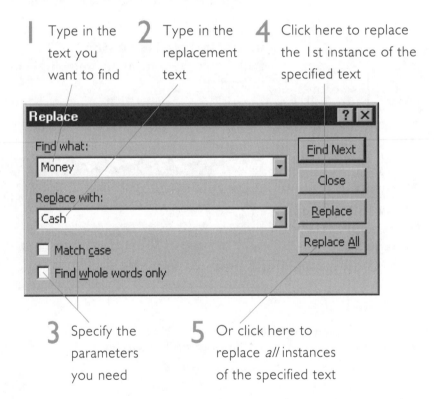

3 Specify the parameters you need

5 Or click here to replace *all* instances of the specified text

Spell-checking

PowerPoint 2000 lets you check text in two ways:

- on-the-fly, as you type in text

- separately, after the text has been entered

 Re step 2 – following this ensures that the word is ignored in this checking session only. (To ignore it forever, carry out step 3 instead.)

Checking text on-the-fly

This is the default. When automatic checking is in force, PowerPoint 2000 flags words it doesn't recognise, using a red underline. If the word or phrase is wrong, right-click in it. Then carry out steps 1, 2, 3 OR 4:

> PowerPoint often provides a list of alternatives. If one is correct, click it; the flagged word is replaced with the correct version

 Re step 3 – PowerPoint maintains a special dictionary (called NEW.DIC). Carry out step 3 if:

1. the flagged word is correct, and;

2. you want PowerPoint to remember it in future spell-checks (by adding it to the NEW dictionary)

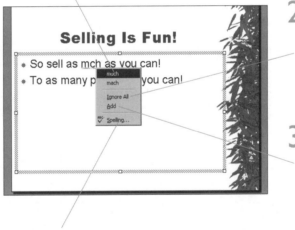

2 Click here if you want the flagged word to stand

3 Click here to have the word added to your user dictionary

4 If the flagged word is wrong but can't be corrected now, click here and complete the resulting dialog (see page 60)

Disabling on-the-fly checking

Pull down the Tools menu and click Options. Activate the Spelling and Style tab, then deselect Check spelling as you type. Click OK.

...cont'd

Re step 1 – if none of the suggestions are correct, type the correct word in the Change to: field then follow step 2.

PowerPoint makes use of two separate dictionaries. One – NEW.DIC – is yours. When you click the Add button (see the tip below), the flagged word is stored in NEW.DIC and recognised in future checking sessions.

You have two further options:

• **Click Add to store the flagged word in NEW.DIC, or;**
• **Click Change All to substitute the suggestion for *all* future instances of the flagged word (only in *this* checking session)**

Checking text separately

To check all the text within the active slide show in one go, pull down the Tools menu and click Spelling. PowerPoint 2000 starts spell-checking the presentation from the present location. When it encounters a word or phrase it doesn't recognise, PowerPoint flags it and produces a special dialog (see below). Usually, it provides alternative suggestions; if one of these is correct, you can opt to have it replace the flagged word. You can do this singly (i.e. just this instance is replaced) or globally (where all future instances – within the current checking session – are replaced).

Alternatively, you can have PowerPoint ignore *this* instance of the flagged word, ignore *all* future instances of the word or add the word to NEW.DIC (see the HOT TIPS). After this, PowerPoint resumes checking.

Carry out step 1 below, then follow step 2. Alternatively, carry out step 3 or 4.

1   If one of the suggestions here is correct, click it, then follow step 2

3   Click here to ignore just this instance

4   Click here to ignore all future instances

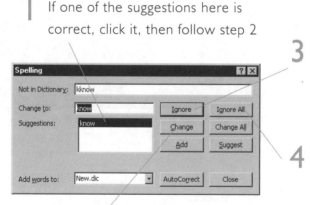

2   Click here to replace this instance

Saving slide shows

It's important to save your work at frequent intervals, in order to avoid data loss in the event of a hardware fault or power interruption.

Saving a document for the first time

Pull down the File menu and click Save. Or press Ctrl+S. Now do the following:

Re step 2 – click any buttons in the Save banner for access to the relevant folders. (For instance, to save files to your Desktop, click Desktop.)

2 Click here; in the drop-down list, click a drive

3 Optional – double-click one or more folders

Re step 3 – carry out this until you reach the correct folder.

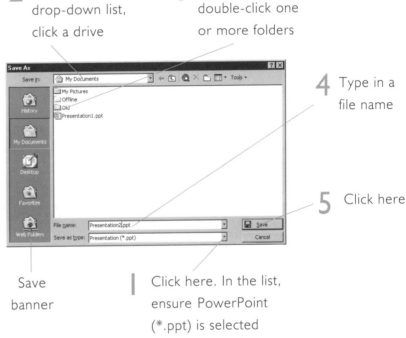

4 Type in a file name

5 Click here

Re step 1 – by default, slide shows are saved in PowerPoint's own current format. To save your slide to other formats (e.g. earlier versions of PowerPoint), simply select the relevant entry.

Save banner

Click here. In the list, ensure PowerPoint (*.ppt) is selected

Saving previously saved presentations

Pull down the File menu and click Save. Or press Ctrl+S. No dialog launches; instead, PowerPoint 2000 saves the latest version of your slide show to disk, overwriting the previous version.

Opening slide shows

We saw earlier that PowerPoint 2000 lets you create new presentations in various ways. You can open these whenever you want.

Pull down the File menu and click Open. Now carry out steps 1–5 below, as appropriate:

Re step 4 – you may have to double-click one or more folders first, to locate the slide show you want to open.

Re steps 1 and 2 – to open a slide show in another format, simply select it in step 2.

To set up a FTP site, click the Look in: field in the Open dialog. In the list, select Add/Modify FTP Locations. Complete the dialog, then click Add. Click OK, then press Esc.

3 Click here. In the drop-down list, click the relevant drive

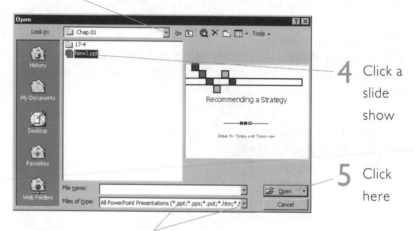

4 Click a slide show

5 Click here

| Make sure All PowerPoint Presentations... is shown. If it isn't, click the arrow and follow step 2

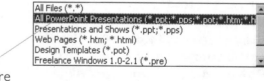

2 Click here

Saving to the Internet

 You can use Windows Explorer to create Web folders (as a shortcut to working with Web servers).

In the Explorer hierarchy, do the following:

Click here

Now activate this icon in the pane on the right:

and follow the on-screen instructions.

 Before you create a Web folder, get details of servers which support Web folders from your:

• **system administrator, or:**
• **Internet Service Provider**

You can save slide shows (usually in HTML – HyperText Markup Language – format) to:

• a pre-established Web folder (Web folders are shortcuts to Web servers)

• a pre-established FTP site on the World Wide Web

(See the DON'T FORGET tips on this and the facing page for how to set up Web folders and FTP sites.)

You can also save HTML files directly to Intranets, using the same techniques.

HTML enhancements

While PowerPoint 2000 preserves its own native format (*.ppt) so that it's identical with the format used by PowerPoint 97, the standard Web format (*.html or *.htm) has had the following changes made:

• it's now a Companion File format (Microsoft regards it as occupying the same status as its proprietary formats)

• it now duplicates the functionality of PowerPoint 2000's proprietary format

• you can edit HTML files from within Internet Explorer 5 (or higher) – to do this, see page 160

• it's now recognised by the Windows Clipboard. This means that data can be copied from Internet Explorer and pasted directly into PowerPoint 2000

• from within PowerPoint 2000, you can preview your work directly in Internet Explorer, before you've saved your work to disk (see page 64)

...cont'd

To publish your slide shows on the Web, you must have a live connection to the Internet.

Before you can save files to Web folders or FTP sites, you must first have carried out the relevant procedures in the DON'T FORGET tips on pages 62-63.

Re step 1 – do one of the following:

- To save to a FTP site, click FTP Locations. Double-click a FTP site, then double-click where you want to save to
- To save to a Web server, click Web Folders. Activate a Web folder

Previewing your work before saving
Pull down the File menu and do the following:

Click here

Your browser now launches, with your work displayed in it.

Saving your work to a Web folder or FTP site
Pull down the File menu and click Save as Web Page. Then do the following:

Click here. In the drop-down list, select a recipient – see the HOT TIP

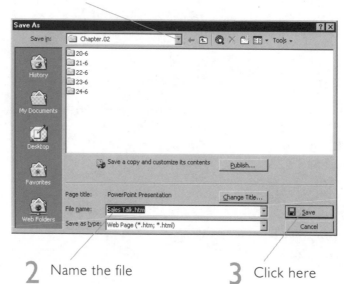

2 Name the file   3 Click here

Slide design

Use this chapter to fine-tune the appearance of slides. You'll learn how to use the Slide and Title masters to ensure your presentations have a consistent look. You'll also discover how to apply and change colour schemes, (and how to copy colour schemes between slides with Format Painter), and go on to apply design templates, two additional techniques for achieving consistency. Finally, you'll add new slide backgrounds; amend slide and handout/note headers and footers; and then save your presentation as a template for future use.

Covers

Chapter Three

Customising slides – an overview

PowerPoint 2000 provides several methods you can use to enhance slide appearance quickly and conveniently. You can:

You can also enhance the appearance of handouts and notes by using the Handout and Notes masters.

- customise Slide masters

- customise Title masters

- apply a new colour scheme

- apply design templates

Slide masters

Slide masters control text placing and formatting, but not content.

In other words, you can amend the appearance or position of text for all slides within a presentation, but not the text itself.

(If you have specific text you want to appear on all slides apart from the first, insert a text box into the Slide master. To do this, use the techniques discussed on page 48.)

Slide masters are control slides which determine the format and position of *all* titles and text on slides (but see the BEWARE tip). You can also insert other objects – e.g. pictures – onto a Slide master; when you do this, they're reproduced (unless you change this) on all slides *after* the first. In this way, if you want a picture – for instance, a company logo – to appear on every slide except the first, you can simply insert it on the Slide master.

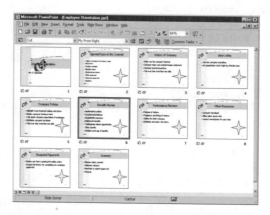

Here, a star (AutoShape) has been added to the Slide master; it appears on every slide apart from the first

Title masters

Title masters perform the same function as Slide masters, but only in respect of the Title (first) slide.

...cont'd

See Chapter 7 for how to work with Handout and Notes masters.

Within any master, you can restore deleted elements. **Pull down the Format menu and do the following:**

- **click Master Layout (re. Slide and Title masters)**
- **click Handout Master Layout (re. Handout masters), or;**
- **click Notes Master Layout (re. Notes masters)** **Now do the following:**

B **Click here**

A **Click any missing element**

Handout masters

You can include the following in Handout masters and have them appear on handouts:

- pictures
- text
- headers/footers
- date/time information
- page numbers

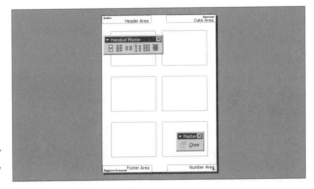

The Handout master

Notes masters

You can include the same components in Notes masters to have them appear on notes.

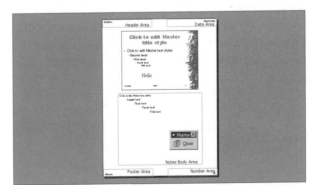

The Notes master

Colour schemes are tailor-made for the design template which hosts them.

If you plan to work on both the Slide and Title masters, work on the Slide master first (because text formatting changes on the Slide master are automatically mirrored in the Title master).

When you apply a design template, any objects you've already applied to the Slide master (e.g. pictures or text boxes) remain.

Colour schemes

Colour schemes are integrated collections of colours which are guaranteed to complement each other. Each colour scheme contains eight balanced colours which are automatically applied to slide elements such as:

- text
- background
- fill

You can apply colour schemes to individual slides, or to the whole of a presentation.

You can also create and use your own colour schemes.

Design templates

Design templates – otherwise known simply as designs – are collections of:

- Slide masters (and often Title masters)
- colour schemes
- specific fonts which complement other elements in the design

When you apply a design template to a slide show (you can only do so to the whole presentation, not to specific slides), it takes precedence over the existing Slide master, Title master and colour scheme. This means that when you create new slides, they automatically assume the characteristics of the new design template, irrespective of any AutoLayouts you may have applied previously.

Summary

Appropriate editing of Slide/Title masters (or the application of a new colour scheme) represents a convenient technique for ensuring your slide show has a uniform appearance and/or content. Applying a new design template is a way of doing both at the same time.

Working with the Slide master

Editing the Slide master is easy and convenient.

Launching the Slide master
Pull down the View menu and do the following:

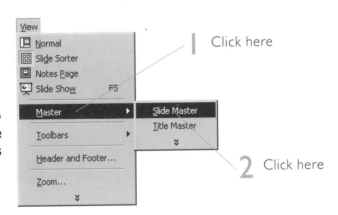

Click here

See Chapter 7 for how to launch the Handout and Notes masters.

2 Click here

The end result:

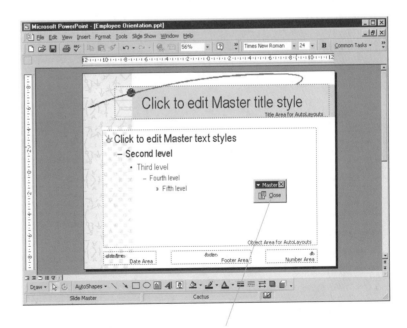

Master toolbar

...cont'd

Editing the Slide master

Do any of the following:

To format text within Slide masters, use the techniques discussed on pages 49-51.

For how to work with headers/ footers, see pages 80-82.

For how to insert pictures into master slides, see Chapter 6.

Click in a text entry, then apply any appropriate formatting enhancements

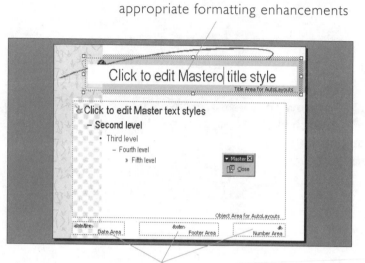

Click in a specialised text box, then apply any appropriate formatting enhancements

Closing the Slide master

When you've finished with the Slide master, refer to the Master toolbar. Do the following to return to the PowerPoint 2000 view you were using before you launched it:

If the Master toolbar isn't on-screen, pull down the View menu and click Toolbars, Master.

Click here

Working with the Title master

Editing the Title master is easy and convenient.

Launching the Title master

Pull down the View menu and do the following:

See Chapter 7 for how to launch the Handout and Notes masters.

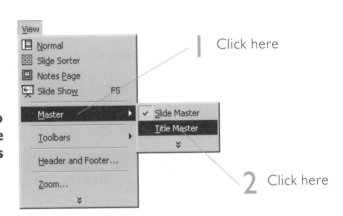

Click here

2 Click here

The end result:

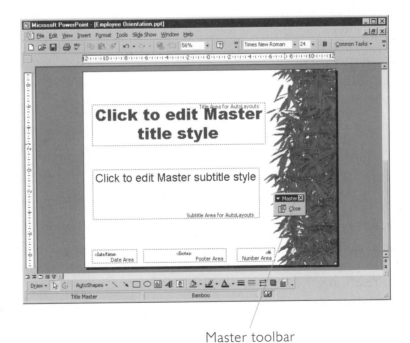

Master toolbar

...cont'd

Editing the Title master

Do any of the following:

For how to format text within Slide masters, use the techniques discussed on pages 49-51.

For how to work with headers/ footers, see pages 80-82.

For how to insert pictures into master Slides, see Chapter 6.

Click in a text entry, then apply any appropriate formatting enhancements

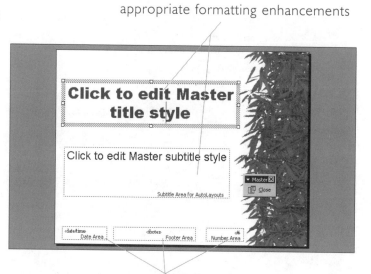

Click in a specialised text box, then apply any appropriate formatting enhancements

Closing the Title master

When you've finished with the Slide master, refer to the Master toolbar. Do the following to return to the PowerPoint 2000 view you were using before you launched it:

If the Master toolbar isn't on-screen, pull down the View menu and click Toolbars, Master.

Click here

Applying colour schemes

Applying a new colour scheme is a quick and effective way to give a presentation a new and consistent look.

Any PowerPoint 2000 presentation automatically has various colour schemes available to it (they're contained in the design template associated with the slide show).

Imposing a colour scheme

If you want to restrict the colour scheme to one or more slides, first do one of the following:

- In Normal view, go to the slide whose colour scheme you want to replace

- In Slide Sorter view, select one or more slides

Now pull down the Format menu and carry out the following action:

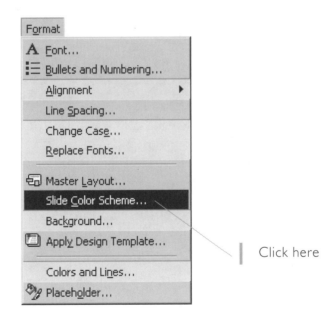

Click here

Carry out steps 2-3 below. If you want to apply the colour scheme to *all* slides within the active presentation, perform step 4. Alternatively, to apply it only to slides pre-selected before step 1, carry out step 5:

2 Ensure this tab is active   4 Click here

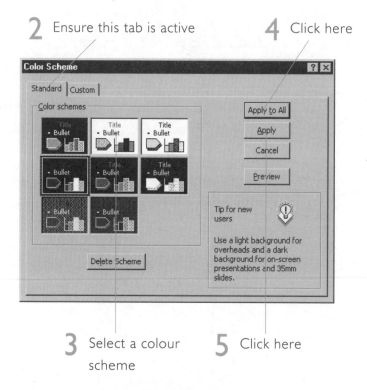

3 Select a colour scheme   5 Click here

PowerPoint 2000 now applies the selected colour scheme.

Previewing colour schemes

To preview the effect of applying a colour scheme, click this button:

immediately after you've carried out step 3 above.

Finally, carry out step 4 OR 5.

Changing colours in a scheme

If you need to, you can change individual colours within a colour scheme. When you do this, all slide objects associated with the colour are automatically updated.

In this way, colours in PowerPoint 2000 are similar to graphics styles within a word processor.

Changing existing colour schemes like this is a way of creating your own – see also the HOT TIP on page 76.

Amending a scheme colour

If you want to restrict the change to one or more slides, first do one of the following:

*   In Normal view, go to the slide whose colour scheme you want to replace

*   In Slide Sorter view, select one or more slides

Now pull down the Format menu and carry out the following steps:

Click here

2 Perform steps 2-3 (to select the colour scheme you want to amend) on page 74

...cont'd

Now carry out steps 3-8 below. Then, if you want to apply the colour scheme changes to *all* slides within the active presentation, perform step 9. Alternatively, to apply them only to slides pre-selected before step 1, carry out step 10:

To see what your slides would look like after the proposed changes, click this button:

3 Click this tab

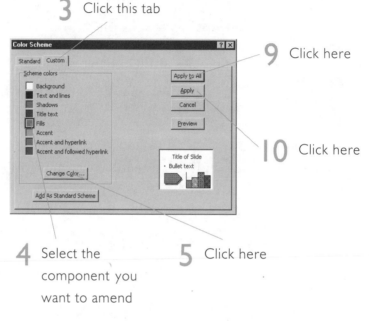

9 Click here

10 Click here

To ensure that the colour changes you've made are saved with the slide show, click the Add as Standard Scheme button before you carry out steps 9 or 10.

4 Select the component you want to amend

5 Click here

6 Ensure this tab is active

If no colours are suitable, ignore steps 6-8. Instead, click the Custom tab. Click a colour in the Colors box, then drag the slider on the right to adjust the brightness. Click OK. Finally, carry out step 9 or 10.

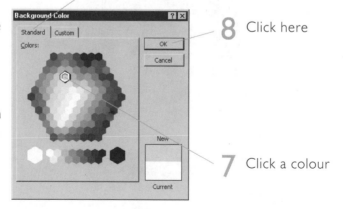

8 Click here

7 Click a colour

Format Painter

PowerPoint 2000 offers a useful shortcut (Format Painter) which enables you to copy a colour scheme:

- from one slide to another

- from one slide to multiple slides

If the Standard toolbar isn't currently on-screen, pull down the View menu and click Toolbars, Standard.

Copying colour schemes

In Slide Sorter view, select the slide whose colour scheme you want to transfer. Refer to the Standard toolbar; carry out step 1 for a single copy, OR step 2 for multiple copies:

| Click here

2 Double-click here

3 Click the slide whose colour scheme you want to copy

Re step 4 – if you followed step 1, click one slide. If you carried out step 2, click more than one.

If you followed step 2, press Esc when you've finished copying the colour scheme.

4 Click the slide(s) you want to apply the colour scheme to

Applying design templates

The Apply Design Template dialog defaults to the folder which holds PowerPoint 2000 templates. If you want to use templates stored in a different drive/ folder combination, select it in the normal way then follow step 2.

You can also use slide shows or HTML files as the basis for a design. Follow step 1. In the dialog, click in the Files of type: field. Click Presentations and Shows or Web Pages... in the list. Then use the Look in: field to locate the relevant drive. Double-click the appropriate folders until you reach the correct one. Now double-click the relevant file.

When you apply a new design template to a presentation, you impose a potent combination of masters and colour schemes. For this reason, designs often represent the best and most convenient way to ensure presentations have an effective and consistent appearance.

Imposing a design

To apply a new design template to the whole of the active presentation, pull down the Format menu and do the following:

Click here

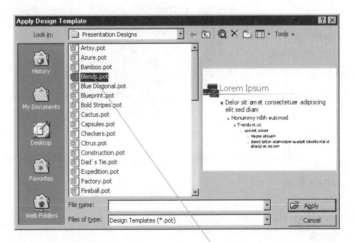

2 Double-click a template

...cont'd

You can also apply new backgrounds to slides.

In Slide Sorter view, select the slide(s) you want to change. Pull down the Format menu and click Background. In the Background dialog, do the following:

Click here

In the drop-down list, select a colour. (Alternatively, click Fill Effects. In the Fill Effects dialog, select the Gradient, Texture or Pattern tab and complete the relevant options. Click OK.)

Back in the Background dialog, click this button:

Apply

Before...

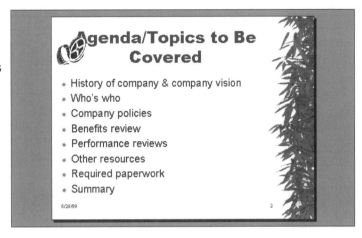

The BAMBOO.POT
template is in force

After...

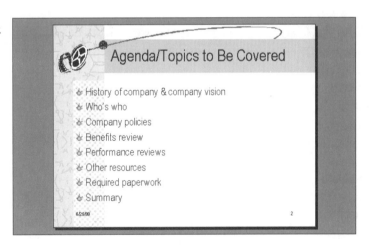

The CACTUS.POT
template has been applied

Working with headers/footers

Headers and footers also appear in handouts and notes – see page 82.

Headers are text elements which appear at the top of each slide within a presentation; footers are elements which appear at the base of each slide.

Typically, you'll use headers and footers to display:

- the date and time of the presentation

- the slide or page number

- information specific to the current presentation

Once you've inserted information in the header and/or footer, you can change the appearance or position of the header and footer on your slides.

To move or reformat header and footer elements, launch the appropriate master (see pages 69 and 71 for how to do this). Select the element(s). Then do either or both of the following:

- **drag them to a new location**
- **apply new formatting characteristics (using the procedures discussed on pages 49-51)**

Using headers/footers in slides

If you want to restrict your amendments to one or more slides, first do one of the following:

- In Normal view, go to the slide whose header you want to change

- In Slide Sorter view, select one or more slides

Now pull down the View menu and do the following:

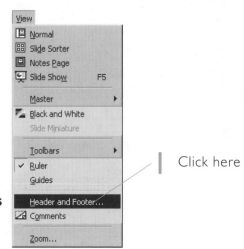

Click here

...cont'd

Carry out step 2 below. If you don't want the date and time to display in the footer area, follow step 3. If you do want the date and time to display, omit step 3; follow step 4 instead. If you want the slide number to display in the footer, perform step 5. To insert specific slide information in the footer, carry out step 6.

Finally, if you want to apply the header/footer changes to *all* slides within the active presentation, perform step 7. Alternatively, to apply them only to slides pre-selected before step 1, carry out step 8:

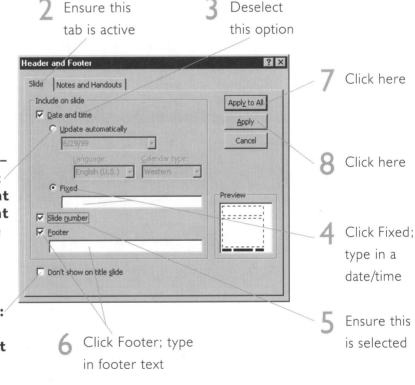

2 Ensure this tab is active

3 Deselect this option

7 Click here

8 Click here

4 Click Fixed; type in a date/time

5 Ensure this is selected

6 Click Footer; type in footer text

Re step 4 – click here: if you want the current date and time to be inserted *automatically*.

Click here: if you don't want your changes to display on the title slide.

...cont'd

Using headers/footers in notes and handouts

Follow step 1 on page 80. Now carry out step 2 below. If you don't want the date and time to display in the footer area, follow step 3. If you do want the date and time to display, omit step 3; follow step 4 instead. If you want the page number to display, perform step 5. To insert specific slide information in the footer, carry out step 6.

Finally, perform step 7 to apply the header/footer changes to *all* slides within the active presentation.

2 Ensure this tab is active

3 Deselect this option

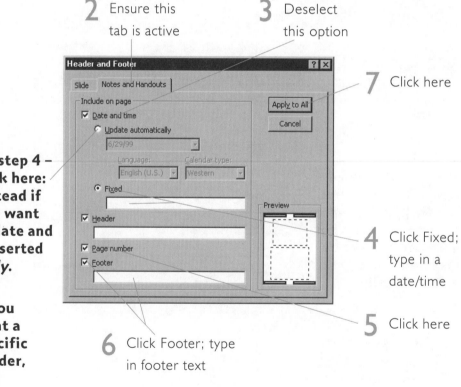

7 Click here

Re step 4 – click here: instead if you want the current date and time to be inserted *automatically*.

If you want a specific header, type it in the Header field.

4 Click Fixed; type in a date/time

5 Click here

6 Click Footer; type in footer text

Saving your work as a template

PowerPoint 2000 lets you save slide shows you've created as templates. When you need to create a new presentation, you can then base it on the template (see pages 37-39 for how to do this). This technique can save you a lot of time and effort.

Templates you create using the procedures outlined below contain:

- masters

- colour schemes

- content (text and pictures)

Be careful you don't save the original slide show after any deletions (unless you want this, of course).

Creating a template

Open the slide show you want to serve as the basis for a template. If necessary, delete text and pictures which you don't want to be included in the template. Pull down the File menu and do the following:

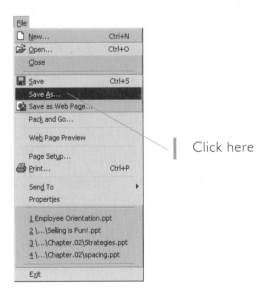

Click here

Carry out the following additional steps:

4 Name the template

5 Click here

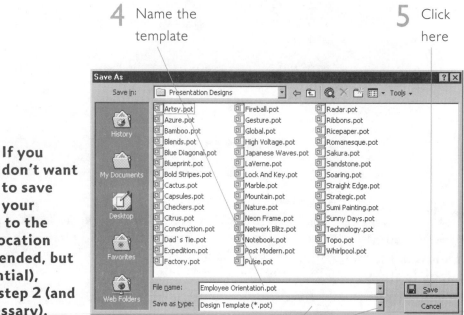

If you don't want to save your template to the default location (recommended, but not essential), perform step 2 (and 3, if necessary). Now use the Save in: box to locate the appropriate drive. Double-click the relevant folder(s) until you reach the correct one. Finally, carry out steps 4-5.

2 Make sure Design Template (*.pot) is shown. If it isn't, click the arrow and follow step 3 below

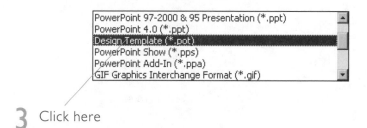

3 Click here

Working with objects

Use this chapter to learn how to create and insert 'objects' (simple or complex graphic elements) in order to make your presentations more visually effective. You'll create lines, curves, rectangles/squares and ellipses/circles. Then you'll move on to create AutoShapes, extraordinarily flexible graphics which are very easy to use. Finally, you'll reformat your objects (especially AutoShapes) in various ways.

Covers

Chapter Four

Objects – an overview

You can use the following method to edit inserted objects (in addition to the techniques discussed on pages 99-106).

Double-click any object to produce the Format AutoShape dialog. Activate the appropriate tab, then make the necessary amendments. (For example, to amend the object's size, click the Size tab and enter new settings in the Height/Width fields...)

Finally, click OK.

You can add a variety of objects to your presentations:

*   lines

*   arrowed lines

*   simple shapes (squares/rectangles and circles/ellipses)

*   curves and freeform curve/line combinations

*   a wide assortment of flexible shapes (known as AutoShapes)

The judicious inclusion of objects in your slide shows makes them more visual and can considerably enhance their effect.

AutoShapes are ready-made shapes you can define and manipulate with just a few mouse clicks. They're readily adjustable, and fall into several categories. These include:

Action Buttons   *Stars and Banners*
Basic Shapes   *Callouts*

When you've inserted objects, you can manipulate them in several ways. You can:

All inserted objects can also be resized/moved with the use of standard Windows mouse techniques.

*   move them

*   resize them

*   rotate/flip them

*   apply a colour/fill

*   apply a shadow

*   make them 3D

*   (in the case of *complex* AutoShapes – see the DON'T FORGET tip on page 87) convert them into other shapes

Creating lines

Technically, all objects you insert in PowerPoint 2000 are AutoShapes. However, this book makes a functional distinction between simple objects (lines, curves etc.) and the more complex AutoShapes discussed on pages 99-106...

PowerPoint 2000 lets you create:

- straight lines

- single-arrowed lines

- double-arrowed lines

- curved lines (see pages 94-96)

- freeform lines (see pages 97-98)

Creating a straight line

First, ensure you're using Normal or Notes Pages view. Refer to the Drawing toolbar and do the following:

Re step 2 – to constrain the new line to 15° increments, hold down one Shift key as you define it.

| Click here

2 Click where you want the line to begin and drag to define the line. Release the mouse button when you've finished

Re step 2 – to define the line outwards (to the left and right) from the starting point, hold down Ctrl as you drag.

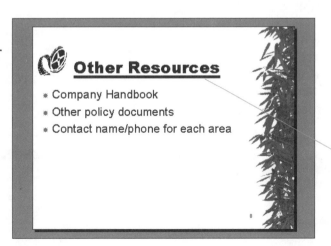

An inserted line

Creating a single-arrowed line

First, ensure you're using Normal or Notes Pages view. Refer to the Drawing toolbar and do the following:

Re step 2 – to constrain the new line to 15° increments, hold down one Shift key as you define it.

Re step 2 – to define the line outwards (to the left and right) from the starting point, hold down Ctrl as you drag.

The lines in these examples have been thickened.

To thicken a line (or other object), select it. Refer to the Drawing toolbar and click this icon:

In the graphic list, select a line weight e.g.

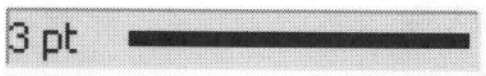

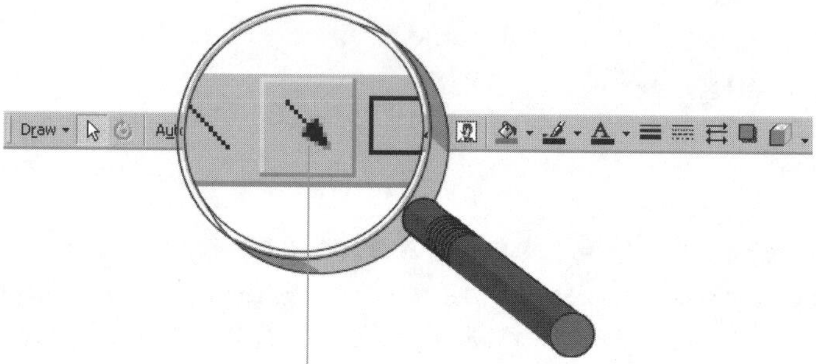

1 Click here

2 Click where you want the arrowed line to begin and drag to define the line. Release the mouse button when you've finished

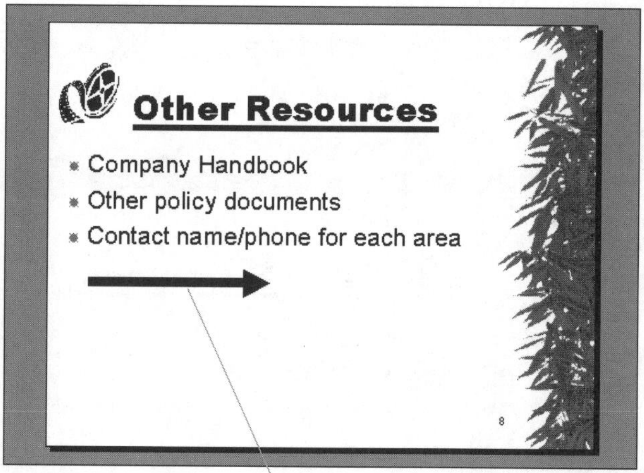

The inserted line

...cont'd

If the Drawing toolbar isn't currently on-screen, pull down the View menu and click Toolbars, Drawing.

Creating a double-arrowed line

First, ensure you're using Normal or Notes Pages view. Refer to the Drawing toolbar and do the following:

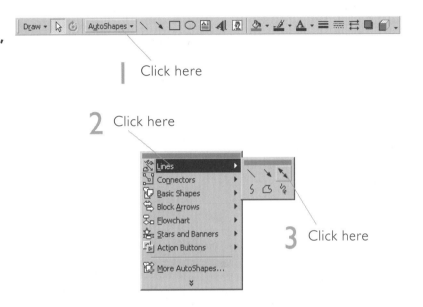

1 Click here

2 Click here

3 Click here

4 Click where you want the arrowed line to begin, then drag to define it. Release the mouse button when you've finished

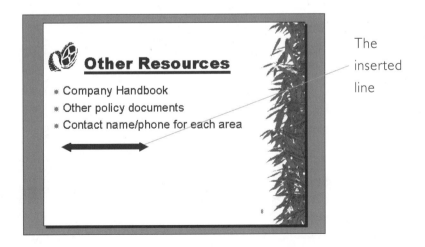

The inserted line

Creating rectangles

 You can use another route to create a rectangle. Follow step 1 above. Then click in your slide where you want the rectangle to begin. PowerPoint 2000 inserts the following:

Ensure this prototype rectangle is selected then resize it appropriately (for how to do this, see 'Resizing AutoShapes' on page 100, or the HOT TIP on page 86).

 To apply fills to objects, follow the techniques described on pages 102-103.

Drawing a rectangle

First, ensure you're using Normal or Notes Pages view. Refer to the Drawing toolbar and do the following:

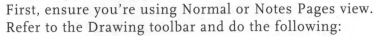

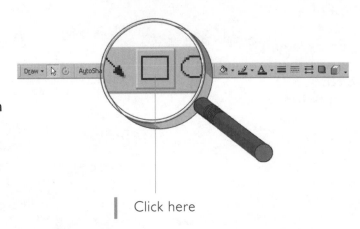

Click here

2 Place the mouse pointer where you want one corner of the rectangle to begin

3 Click and hold down the left mouse button, then drag to create the rectangle

4 Release the mouse button

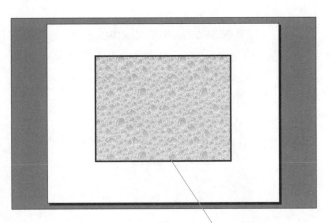

An inserted rectangle, plus a textured fill

Creating squares

Drawing a square

First, ensure you're using Normal or Notes Pages view. Refer to the Drawing toolbar and do the following:

You can use another route to create a square. Follow step 1 above. Then click in your slide where you want the square to begin. PowerPoint 2000 inserts the following:

Ensure this prototype square is selected then resize it appropriately (for how to do this, see 'Resizing AutoShapes' on page 100), holding down Shift as you do so.

To apply fills to objects, follow the techniques described on pages 102-103.

Click here

2 Place the mouse pointer where you want one corner of the square to begin

3 Hold down Shift. Click and hold down the left mouse button, then drag to create the square

4 Release the mouse button and Shift

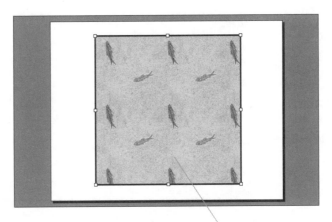

An inserted square, plus a textured fill

Creating ellipses

You can use another route to create an ellipse. Follow step 1 above. Then click in your slide where you want the ellipse to begin. PowerPoint 2000 inserts the following:

Ensure this prototype ellipse is selected then resize it appropriately (for how to do this, see 'Resizing AutoShapes' on page 100, or the HOT TIP on page 86).

To apply fills to objects, follow the techniques described on pages 102-103.

Drawing an ellipse

First, ensure you're using Normal or Notes Pages view. Refer to the Drawing toolbar and do the following:

Click here

2   Place the mouse pointer where you want one corner of the ellipse to begin

3   Click and hold down the left mouse button, then drag to create the ellipse

4   Release the mouse button

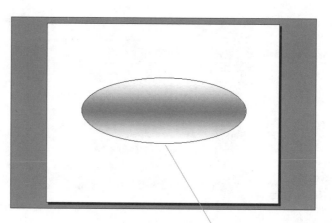

An inserted ellipse, plus a gradient fill

Creating circles

Drawing a circle

 You can use another route to create a circle. Follow step 1 above. Then click in your slide where you want the circle to begin. PowerPoint 2000 inserts the following:

First, ensure you're using Normal or Notes Pages view. Refer to the Drawing toolbar and do the following:

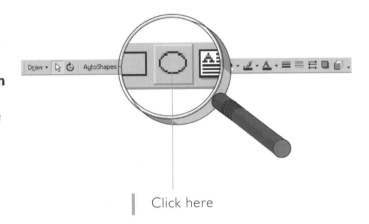

Click here

Ensure this prototype circle is selected then resize it appropriately (for how to do this, see 'Resizing AutoShapes' on page 100), holding down Shift as you do so.

2 Place the mouse pointer where you want one corner of the circle to begin

3 Hold down Shift. Click and hold down the left mouse button, then drag to create the circle

4 Release the mouse button and Shift

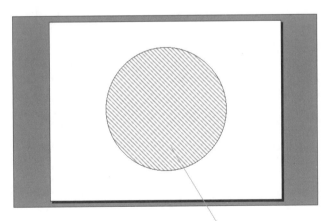

 To apply fills to objects, follow the techniques described on pages 102-103.

An inserted circle, plus a pattern fill

Creating Bezier curves

PowerPoint 2000 lets you create three types of curves:

Bezier   provides great control and
                                    accuracy

Freeform   freehand curve/line
                                    combinations without jagged
                                    edges

Scribble   a lifelike imitation of freehand
                                    drawing

Defining Bezier curves

If you need to create curves in your presentations, this is
the technique you'll normally use. In effect, you provide
PowerPoint 2000 with details of where two (or more)
points should be placed and it creates the appropriate
curve(s) between them, smoothly and efficiently.

First, ensure you're using Normal or Notes Pages view.
Refer to the Drawing toolbar and do the following:

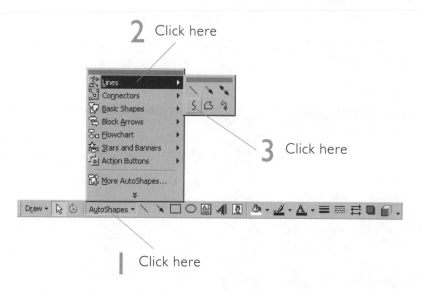

2 Click here

3 Click here

1 Click here

Now carry out the following additional steps:

4 Place the mouse pointer where
you want the curve to begin

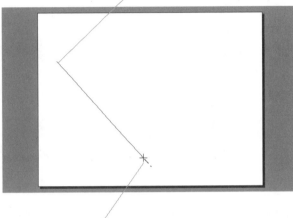

5 Drag out the first curve
coordinate, then left-click once

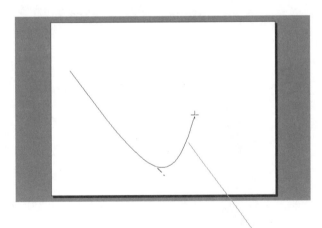

6 Move the mouse pointer to complete
the 1st curve, then left-click once

...cont'd

7 Optional – move the mouse pointer to define another curve, then left-click

Re step 9 – use a different procedure if you want to produce a closed shape e.g.

Simply left-click once near the curve start point.

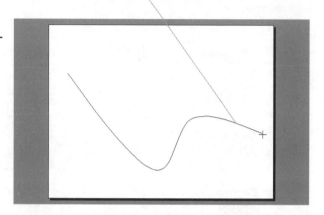

8 Repeat step 7 as often as required

9 When you've finished defining curves, double-click once

A completed Bezier curve:

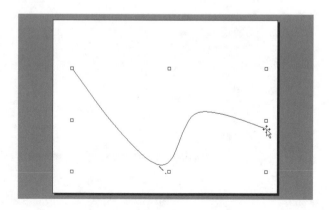

Creating freeform curves/lines

Use the Freeform tool to create objects with both curved and straight components.

Using the Freeform tool

First, ensure you're using Normal or Notes Pages view. Refer to the Drawing toolbar and do the following:

2 Click here

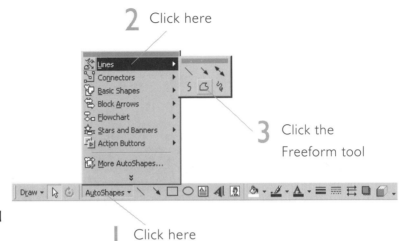

3 Click the Freeform tool

Click here

You should perform step 5 OR 6, as appropriate. (Do so as often as required.)

4 Place the mouse pointer where you want the object to begin

5 Click and hold down the left mouse button, then drag to create a freehand shape, OR:

Re step 7 – use a different procedure if you want to produce a closed shape e.g.

6 Left-click, then move the mouse pointer and left-click again, to create a straight line

7 When you've finished drawing, double-click once

Simply left-click once near the object start point.

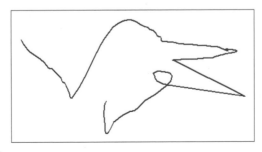

A freeform curve/line combination

Creating curves with Scribble

Use the Scribble tool to create objects which look as if they were drawn with a pen.

Using the Scribble tool

First, ensure you're using Normal or Notes Pages view. Refer to the Drawing toolbar and do the following:

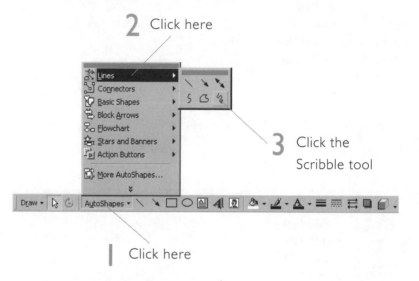

2 Click here

3 Click the Scribble tool

| Click here

4 Place the mouse pointer where you want your curve to begin

Re step 6 – use a different procedure if you want to produce a closed shape e.g.

5 Click and hold down the left mouse button, then drag out the curve

6 Release the mouse button when you've finished

Simply left-click once near the object start point.

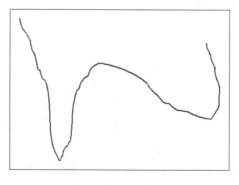

A curve created with Scribble

Creating AutoShapes

You can easily add text to inserted AutoShapes. Right-click the AutoShape. In the menu, click Add Text. The insertion point appears inside the figure; type in the text. Click outside the AutoShape.

AutoShapes represent an extraordinarily flexible and easy-to-use way to insert a wide variety of shapes into your presentations. Once inserted, they can be:

- resized

- rotated/flipped

- coloured/filled

- converted into other shapes

Inserting an AutoShape

First, ensure you're using Normal or Notes Pages view. Refer to the Drawing toolbar and do the following:

Changes you make to an AutoShape also affect any inserted text.

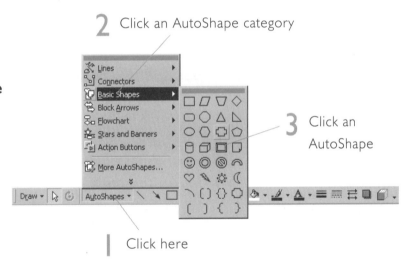

2 Click an AutoShape category

3 Click an AutoShape

Click here

You can use a shortcut to insert AutoShapes. Follow steps 1-3, then simply click where you want the AutoShape inserted. Now resize it appropriately – see page 100.

4 Place the mouse pointer where you want your AutoShape to begin

5 Click and hold down the left mouse button, then drag out the shape

6 Release the mouse button when you've finished

Resizing/rotating AutoShapes

To rotate in 90° stages, don't follow steps 1 or 2. Instead, click the Draw button. In the menu, click Rotate or Flip. In the sub-menu, click Rotate Left or Rotate Right.

You can make use of extra, Web-based AutoShapes.

Go to the relevant slide in Normal view, then follow step 1 on page 99. Click More AutoShapes. In the dialog, activate any of these categories:

- Web Backgrounds
- Web Banners
- Web Bullets & Buttons
- Web Dividers
- Web Elements

Now right-click the shape you want to use. In the menu, click Insert. Finally, click this button:

Resizing AutoShapes

Select the AutoShape. Now do the following:

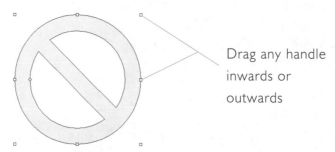

Drag any handle inwards or outwards

Rotating AutoShapes

Select the AutoShape. Now refer to the Drawing toolbar and do the following:

1 Click here

2 Position the mouse pointer over one of the handles – it changes to a rotation symbol

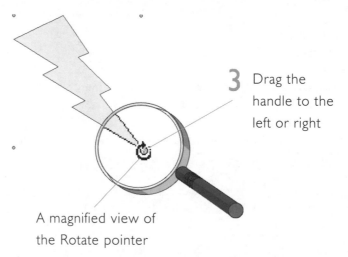

3 Drag the handle to the left or right

A magnified view of the Rotate pointer

Flipping AutoShapes

In Normal or Notes Pages view, select the AutoShape. Refer to the Drawing toolbar and do the following:

You can use this technique with any drawing object created in PowerPoint 2000.

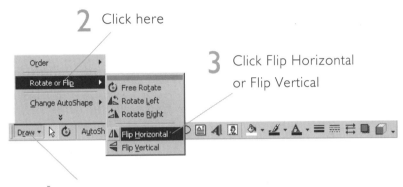

2 Click here

3 Click Flip Horizontal or Flip Vertical

Click here

Most AutoShapes have a special handle:

Magnified view of AutoShape handle

Dragging on this changes the AutoShape's properties:

Flipping in action:

An AutoShape object

The same object after vertical flip

Filling AutoShapes

Applying colour fills to AutoShapes

In Normal or Notes Pages view, select the AutoShape. Refer to the Drawing toolbar, then carry out step 1. If the available colours are suitable, perform step 2. If not, carry out steps 3 and 4 instead:

 You can use these techniques with any drawing object created in PowerPoint 2000.

 Use any of the procedures here and on the facing page to adjust existing fills.

 Re step 4 – if you want to define your own colour, click the Custom tab instead. Click a colour in the Colors: box. Drag the slider on the right to adjust the brightness. Finally, omit step 5; instead, click OK.

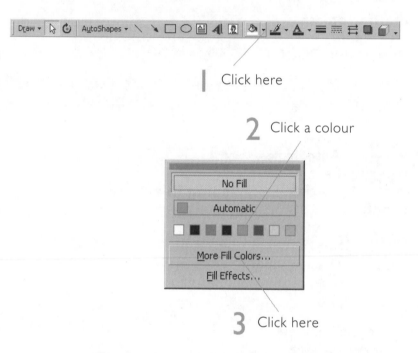

| Click here

2 Click a colour

3 Click here

4 Ensure this tab is active

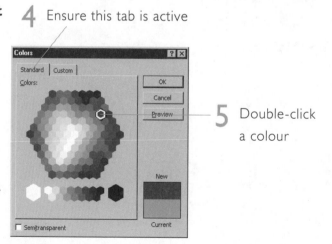

5 Double-click a colour

...cont'd

Re step 3 –
click
Gradient
to apply a
graduated fill,
Texture a textured
fill or Pattern a
basic pattern.

Applying complex fills to AutoShapes

In Normal or Notes Pages view, select the AutoShape. Now
do the following:

Click here

You can
also use
pictures as
fills e.g.

Select the Picture
tab in step 3. Click
the Select Picture
button. Now use the
Select Picture
dialog to locate and
double-click the
relevant image.
Finally, carry out
step 5.

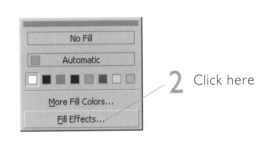

2 Click here

3 Click a tab (see
the HOT TIPS)

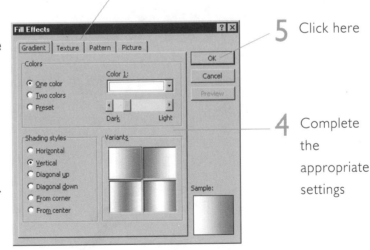

5 Click here

4 Complete
the
appropriate
settings

Re step 4 –
the
available
options
depend on which tab
you've selected in
step 3.

Shadowing AutoShapes

You can use these techniques with any drawing object created in PowerPoint 2000.

In Normal or Notes Pages view, select the relevant AutoShape. Refer to the Drawing toolbar and do the following:

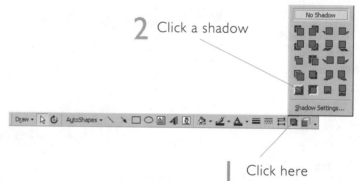

2 Click a shadow

Click here

To vary the shadow colour, select the object. Follow step 1. In the pop-up Shadow list, click the Shadow Settings button. The Shadow Settings toolbar launches. Do the following:

Click here

In the drop-down list, click a colour. (Alternatively, click More Shadow Colors in the list, then carry out steps 4-5 on page 102.)

Shadowing in action:

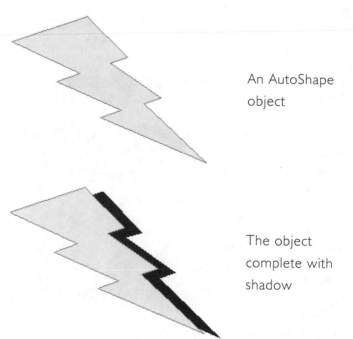

An AutoShape object

The object complete with shadow

Making AutoShapes 3D

In Normal or Notes Pages view, select the AutoShape. Refer to the Drawing toolbar and do the following:

You can use these techniques with any drawing object created in PowerPoint 2000.

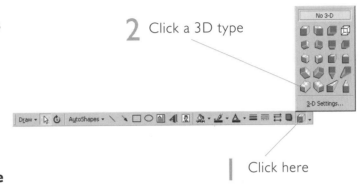

2 Click a 3D type

Click here

To vary the 3D colour, select the object. Follow step 1. In the pop-up 3D list, click the 3-D Settings button. The 3-D Settings toolbar launches. Do the following:

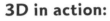

Click here

In the drop-down list, click a colour. (Alternatively, click More 3-D Colors in the list, then carry out steps 4-5 on page 102.)

3D in action:

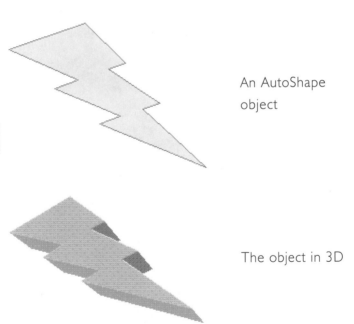

An AutoShape object

The object in 3D

Converting AutoShapes

You can convert AutoShapes from one type to another.

In Normal or Notes Pages view, select the AutoShape. Refer to the Drawing toolbar and do the following:

You can use this technique with any drawing object created in PowerPoint 2000.

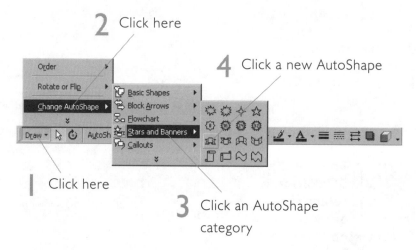

2 Click here

4 Click a new AutoShape

Click here

3 Click an AutoShape category

Conversion in action:

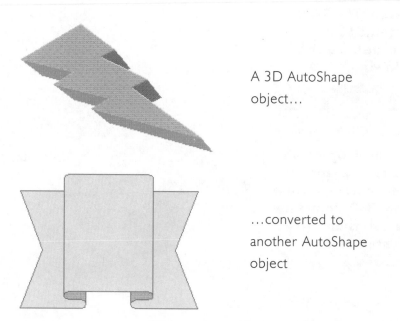

A 3D AutoShape object...

...converted to another AutoShape object

Working with charts

Charts improve slide impact. Use this chapter to learn how to create and insert new charts. You can do this from within PowerPoint 2000 itself with the help of the Datasheet (an inbuilt mini-spreadsheet), or you can base charts on imported data in a variety of external formats. Once you've created charts, you'll learn how to allocate a new chart type. Finally, you'll discover how to reformat the various chart components.

Covers

Chapter Five

Charts – an overview

PowerPoint 2000 makes it easy to insert charts into your presentations. You can do this in two ways:

- by double-clicking chart placeholders (if the slide you're inserting the chart into has had the appropriate AutoLayout applied to it)

- by using a menu route

When you insert a chart, the data on which it's based is displayed in a special window called the Datasheet. The Datasheet can be regarded as a mini version of a typical spreadsheet, and contains sample data which you can easily amend.

Once you've inserted a chart, you can:

- edit the data

- reformat the Datasheet

- import data from a variety of external sources, including Microsoft Excel files

- apply a new chart type/sub-type

- reformat chart objects

When you create or work with charts in PowerPoint 2000, you're actually running a separate program: Microsoft Graph.

Graph runs seamlessly within the PowerPoint 2000 environment (but note that, unlike PowerPoint itself, its menus are not personalised i.e. entries aren't promoted or demoted according to frequency of use).

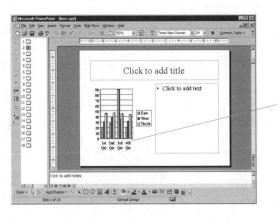

An inserted chart, with sample data

Chart components

PowerPoint 2000 offers 14 overall chart types. There are also numerous sub-types (variants on a theme). In addition, PowerPoint 2000 charts are very customisable: they can contain a wide variety of features/components. The illustration below shows the main ones:

Most charts do not contain all of these elements (they would simply become too cluttered); they're shown here for illustration purposes.

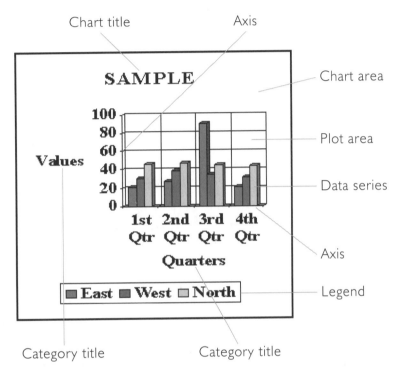

Chart title   Axis

Chart area

Plot area

Data series

Axis

Legend

Category title   Category title

Terminology...

A data series is a group of related values taken from a Datasheet row (horizontal) or column (vertical). In this chart, there are three: East, West and North. (For more information on the use of the Datasheet, see pages 112-114.)

The distinctions listed here between the X, Y and Z axes are sometimes blurred.

Axes are lines which border the chart area; chart values are measured against axes. In most charts, the Y (Value) axis is vertical, while the X (Category) axis is horizontal.

Some charts also have a Z (Time) axis which allows values to be related to time.

Inserting charts

The placeholder route

In Normal view, display the slide into which you want to insert the chart. Carry out the following steps:

Chart placeholder

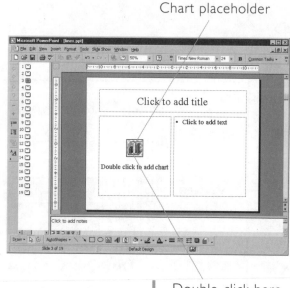

Double-click here

Re step 2 – for how to complete the Datasheet, see page 112.

2 Complete the Datasheet, then click anywhere in the slide

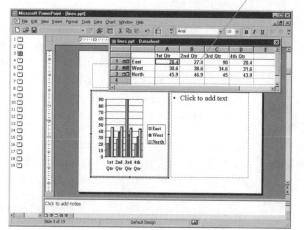

...cont'd

Inserting charts – the menu route

In Normal view, display the slide into which you want to insert the chart. Pull down the Insert menu and carry out the following steps:

Click here

Re step 2 – for how to complete the Datasheet, see page 112.

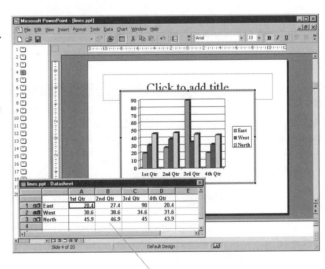

2 Complete the Datasheet, then click anywhere in the slide

Editing chart data

After you've created a chart, and irrespective of the way you created it, you can revise the data on which it's based. PowerPoint 2000 makes this process easy and convenient.

Amending data

Right-click over the chart you want to amend. Do the following:

Cells are formed where rows and columns intersect:

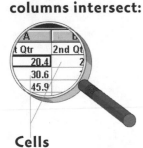

Cells

Click here

1

Click here

2

PowerPoint 2000 launches the Datasheet. Perform any of steps 3-5, then carry out step 6:

3 Amend the axis titles

If you want to hide the Datasheet while leaving the chart active, pull down the View menu and click Datasheet. **(You can also use this procedure to reveal the Datasheet, if appropriate.)**

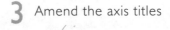

			A	B	C	D	E
			1st Qtr	2nd Qtr	3rd Qtr	4th Qtr	
1		East	20.4	27.4	90	20.4	
2		West	30.6	38.6	34.6	31.6	
3		North	45.9	46.9	45	43.9	
4							

lines.ppt - Datasheet

4 Amend the data series titles

5 Amend the chart values, as appropriate

6 When you've finished, click outside the Datasheet

Reformatting the Datasheet

Formatting changes you make to the Datasheet have no effect on the way your data is represented in the associated chart.

To a limited extent, you can customise how the Datasheet presents information. You can:

*   change the typeface/type size

*   specify how numbers display (e.g. you can set the number of decimal points)

Applying a typeface/type size

Double-click the relevant chart. If the Datasheet isn't visible, pull down the View menu and click Datasheet. Pull down the Format menu and click Font. Carry out step 1 and/or 2 below, as appropriate. Finally, perform step 3:

Click a font

You can also embolden and/or italicise text.
Click one of the options here: before you carry out step 3.

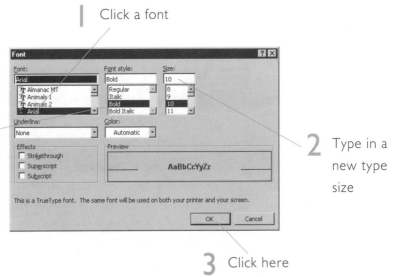

2 Type in a new type size

3 Click here

The end result:

		A	B	C	D	E
		1st Qtr	2nd Qtr	3rd Qtr	4th Qtr	
1	*East*	20.4	27.4	90	20.4	
2	*West*	30.6	38.6	34.6	31.6	
3	*North*	45.9	46.9	45	43.9	
4						

lines.ppt - Datasheet

The font has been italicised

To select multiple cells, first click the cell which forms the upper-left boundary of the cells you want to select. Hold down the mouse button and drag over the remaining cells. Release the mouse button.

Applying a number format

Double-click the relevant chart. (If the Datasheet isn't visible, pull down the View menu and click Datasheet.) Select the cells you want to amend, then pull down the Format menu and carry out step 1 below. Perform step 2 and/or 3, as appropriate. Finally, perform step 4:

| Click here

To select a single cell, simply click in it.

2 Click a number format

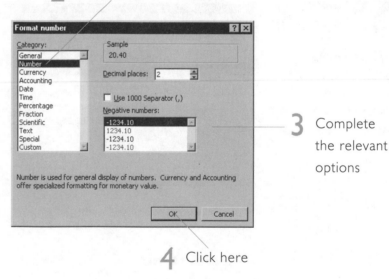

3 Complete the relevant options

Re step 3 – the available options depend on the number format chosen in step 2.

4 Click here

The end result:

		A	B	C	D	E
		1st Qtr	2nd Qtr	3rd Qtr	4th Qtr	
1	East	20	27	90	20	
2	West	31	39	35	32	
3	North	46	47	45	44	
4						

With 0 decimal places

Importing data from Excel

Most database and spreadsheet programs readily export data as text files (data files which lack formatting codes). There are different types. For example, units of data can be differentiated ('delimited') by:

- **commas (probably the most common)**
- **tabs**
- **spaces**

You can have PowerPoint 2000 create charts from third-party data. You can import:

- Microsoft Excel files
- Lotus 1-2-3 files
- text files, also known as 'delimited' or CSV (Comma Separated Value) files

Importing Excel data

Within Normal view, go to the slide in which you want the new chart created. Pull down the Insert menu and click Chart; PowerPoint 2000 inserts a new chart with sample data and launches the Datasheet. If you want the inserted data to begin in any cell other than the upper left, click it. Pull down the Edit menu and click Import File. Now carry out the following:

Click any entry here: for a useful shortcut.
(For instance, to import data from a file on your Desktop, click Desktop...)

2 Click here. In the drop-down list, click the drive which hosts the Excel file

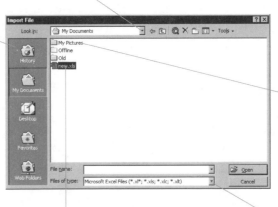

3 Optional – double-click one or more folders

Perform step 3 till you reach the correct folder.

4 Double-click the file you want to import

1 Click here; select Microsoft Excel Files... in the list

...cont'd

PowerPoint 2000 now launches a special dialog. Carry out the following steps:

Re step 5 – data in Excel workbooks (files) is organised into individual worksheets.
(For more on Excel terminology, see 'Excel 2000 in easy steps'.)

5 Select an Excel worksheet

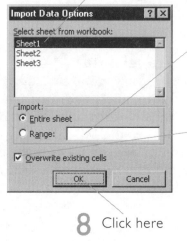

6 If you only want to import specific cells, type in the relevant range

7 Optional – deselect this if you don't want the contents of existing cells overwritten

8 Click here

Re step 6 – type in the start and end cell addresses, separated by a colon.
For instance, to chart only cells H8 to J11, type:
H8:J11

PowerPoint 2000 now creates a new chart based on the imported data.

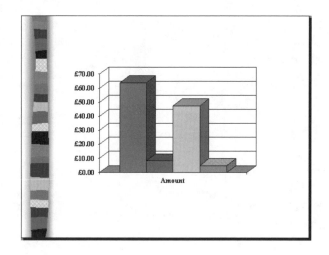

A (simple) inserted chart based on Excel data

Importing data from 1-2-3

Importing 1-2-3 data

Within Normal view, go to the slide in which you want the new chart created. Pull down the Insert menu and click Chart; PowerPoint 2000 inserts a new chart with sample data and launches the Datasheet. If you want the inserted data to begin in any cell other than the upper left, click it. Pull down the Edit menu and click Import File. Now carry out the following:

2 Click here. In the drop-down list, click the drive which hosts the 1-2-3 file

Click any entry here:
for a
useful
shortcut.
(For instance, to import data from a file on your Desktop, click Desktop...)

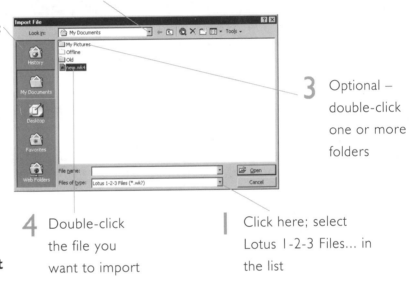

3 Optional – double-click one or more folders

Perform step 3 till you reach the correct folder.

4 Double-click the file you want to import

1 Click here; select Lotus 1-2-3 Files... in the list

In the case of Lotus 1-2-3 files, no further dialog launches. This means that you can only import the *whole* of a 1-2-3 file: you can't specify a cell range for inclusion within PowerPoint 2000.

If you only want to import a cell range, create a copy of the relevant 1-2-3 file and delete the unwanted cells within 1-2-3 itself. Then follow steps 1-4 to import the restricted file.

Importing data from text files

Within Normal view, go to the slide in which you want the new chart created. Pull down the Insert menu and click Chart; PowerPoint 2000 inserts a new chart with sample data and launches the Datasheet. If you want the inserted data to begin in any cell other than the upper left, click it. Pull down the Edit menu and click Import File. Now carry out the following:

2 Click here. In the drop-down list, click the drive which hosts the text file

Click any entry here: for a useful shortcut.
(For instance, to import data from a file on your Desktop, click Desktop...)

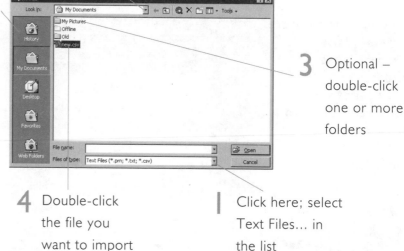

3 Optional – double-click one or more folders

Perform step 3 till you reach the correct folder.

4 Double-click the file you want to import

1 Click here; select Text Files... in the list

PowerPoint 2000 now launches a special wizard.

Complete each stage in line with the instructions on pages 119-120. However, you should note the following:

- PowerPoint 2000 auto-completes most of the settings in the wizard (and previews changes)

- only change these automatic settings if you're sure they're not suitable

...cont'd

Completing the Text Import Wizard

Carry out the following additional steps:

5 Optional – select another file type

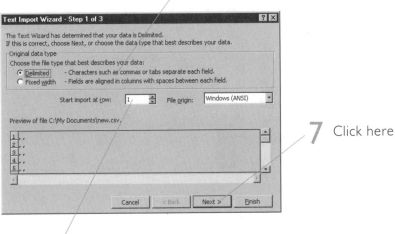

7 Click here

Re step 8 – if you pick the incorrect delimiter, the data in the Preview section will look wrong e.g.

6 Optional – specify the row where the import begins

8 Optional – specify another delimiter

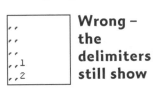

Wrong – the delimiters still show

Right – they're invisible

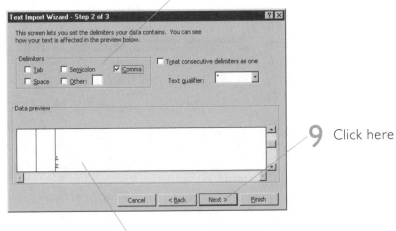

9 Click here

Preview section

...cont'd

Carry out the following additional steps:

Repeat steps 10-11 for as many columns as you need to amend.

Re step 13 – you need to select a separator which is identical to the decimal separator used in the original text file i.e. if the separator is a comma, choose the same.

(If in doubt, leave PowerPoint's choice unaltered.)

Re step 14 – you need to select a separator which is identical to the thousands separator used in the text file i.e. if the separator is a comma, choose the same.

(If in doubt, leave PowerPoint's choice unaltered.)

11 Optional – select a data format

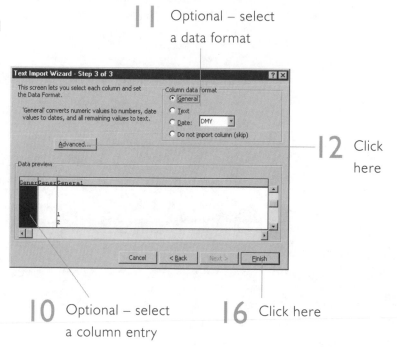

12 Click here

10 Optional – select a column entry

16 Click here

13 Click here; select a decimal separator

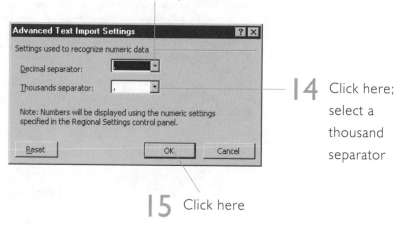

14 Click here; select a thousand separator

15 Click here

Applying a new chart type

After you've inserted a chart, you can change the chart type. There are 14 overall chart types. Some of the most commonly used are:

• Bar

• Pie

• Line

• Area

All of the 14 types have a minimum of 2 sub-types associated with them; most have 6 or more. Often, the available sub-types include 3D alternatives:

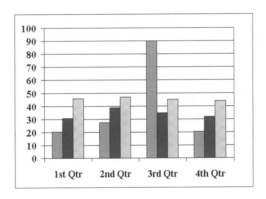

A 2-D Column graph...

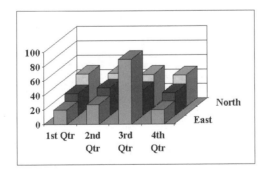

And one of its 3-D sub-types

Changing chart types

Double-click the relevant chart. Then pull down the Chart menu and do the following:

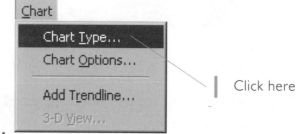

Click here

If you want, you can apply customised chart types (there are 20 to choose from). These are professionally designed formats which also incorporate:

- **colours**
- **patterns**
- **legends and other chart components**

To apply a custom type, don't follow step 2. Instead, activate the Custom Types tab. Then carry out steps 3 and 5 (omit 4 – custom charts don't have sub-types).

2 Ensure this tab is active

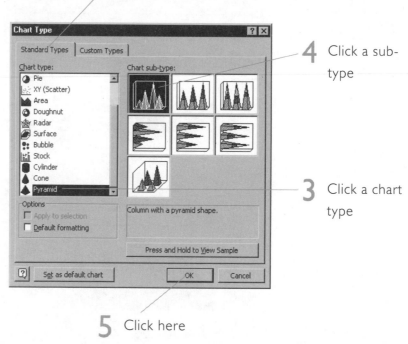

4 Click a sub-type

3 Click a chart type

5 Click here

Colouring chart components

After you've inserted a chart, you can easily vary the formatting. You can select specific chart objects and:

The precise formatting changes you can carry out depend on the object selected.

- apply a colour

- apply a texture/pattern as a fill

- change the line width/border style

- apply a new typeface/type size

Applying a colour

In Normal view, go to the slide which hosts the chart you want to amend. Double-click the chart. Now do the following:

If you're recolouring text (e.g. the textual component of an axis, or a legend), follow step 1 but ignore steps 2-4. In the dialog, select the Font tab. Click the Color: box, then select a colour in the list. Click OK.

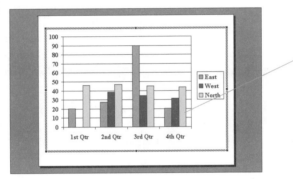

Double-click the component you want to recolour (here, a data series)

2 Ensure this tab is active

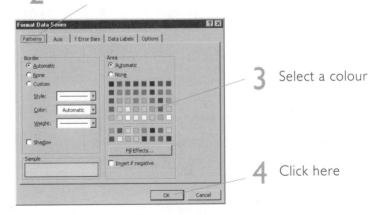

3 Select a colour

4 Click here

Filling chart components

Applying a fill

In Normal view, go to the slide which hosts the chart you want to amend. Double-click the chart. Now double-click the chart component you want to fill. Carry out the following steps:

Re step 3 – click Gradient to apply a graduated fill, Texture a textured fill or Pattern a basic pattern.

You can also use pictures as fills.
Select the Picture tab in step 3. Click the Select Picture button. Now use the Select Picture dialog to locate and double-click the relevant image.
Finally, carry out step 5.

Re step 4 – the available options depend on which tab you've selected in step 3.

1 Ensure this tab is active

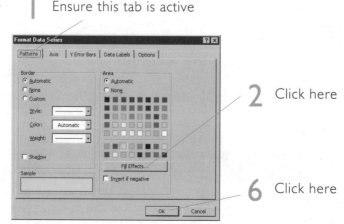

2 Click here

6 Click here

3 Click a tab (see the HOT TIPS)

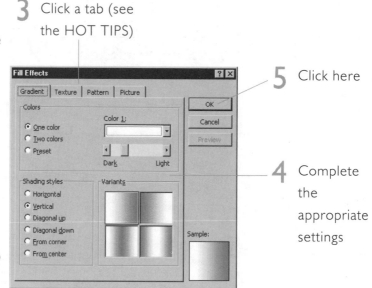

5 Click here

4 Complete the appropriate settings

Bordering chart components

Changing the line width/border style

In Normal view, go to the slide which hosts the chart you want to amend. Double-click the chart. Now double-click the chart component you want to reformat. Carry out step 1 below. Follow 2-3 to apply a line style; 4-5 to apply a line colour; and/or 6-7 to specify a line thickness.

Finally, perform step 8:

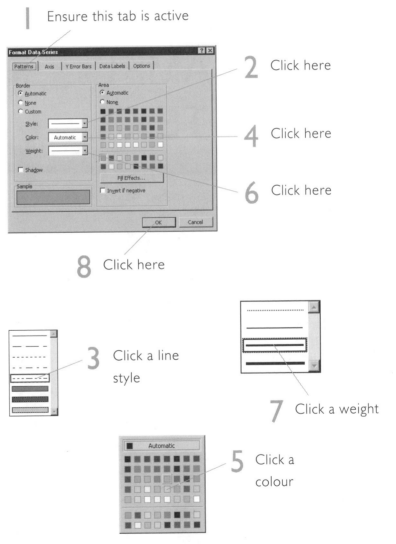

Ensure this tab is active

2 Click here

4 Click here

6 Click here

8 Click here

3 Click a line style

7 Click a weight

5 Click a colour

Formatting text components

To align text, select it within the relevant text box. Pull down the Format menu and click **Alignment**. In the sub-menu, select an alignment.

Re step 1 – this affects all text within the text object. To limit the changes to specific text, select it first. Then right-click over the text and carry out step 2. Perform steps 3-4, as appropriate. Finally, carry out step 5.

You can also embolden and/or italicise text. Click one of the options in the Font style: field before you carry out step 5.

Applying a typeface/type size

In Normal view, go to the slide which hosts the chart you want to amend. Double-click the chart. Now carry out steps 1-2. Follow steps 3-4, as appropriate, then perform step 5:

1 Right-click anywhere on the text frame (but not *inside*)

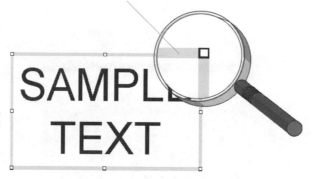

2 In the menu, click Font

3 Select a font

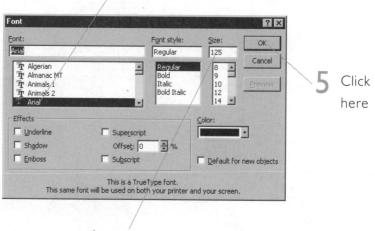

5 Click here

4 Enter a new type size

Using multimedia

Use this chapter to learn how to insert clip art and pictures into slides. In the course of doing this, you'll learn about the various graphics formats (bitmap and vector) which PowerPoint 2000 recognises and translates, and you'll rescale, crop and recolour images. You'll also learn to organise clips in the Gallery, and discover how to insert sound and film clips into slides. Finally, you'll download clips directly from the World Wide Web.

Covers

Chapter Six

Multimedia – an overview

You can add clip art with the use of slide placeholders – see page 130.

You can animate any slide objects (including text) – see page 141.

You can also use the Gallery to organise clips, by:

- **applying categories to clips**
- **renaming or deleting categories**
- **searching for specific clips**
- **adding new clips**
- **removing unwanted clips**

PowerPoint 2000 lets you enhance presentations in a variety of ways. You can add:

- clip art

- third-party pictures

- sound clips

- video clips

Once you've inserted clip art and pictures, you can also animate them.

You can import sound clips, video clips and clip art via the Clip Gallery. This is a computerised scrapbook which helps you access (and organise) multimedia files. You don't have to use the Clip Gallery to insert these into slides, but it does make the process much easier and more convenient.

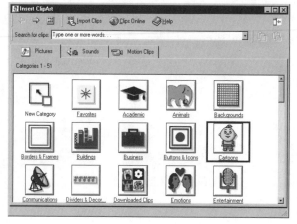

The Clip Gallery Home screen

To return to the Home screen when you're previewing clips, click this button:

You can also add third-party pictures to your slides. These can be:

- output from other programs (e.g. drawings and illustrations)

- commercial clip art

- photographs

Inserting clip art

To have an image appear on every slide except the first, insert it into the slide master.

Pull down the View menu and click Master, Slide Master. Now follow steps 1-4 here OR steps 1-6 on page 139.

To return to the active slide, do the following:

Click here

You can insert clip art into slide shows in two ways:

• with the Office Clip Gallery

• via a separate dialog

Inserting clip art via the Clip Gallery

In Normal or Notes Page views, go to the slide into which you want the clip art added. Pull down the Insert menu and click Picture, Clip Art. Now carry out the following steps:

1 Ensure this tab is activated

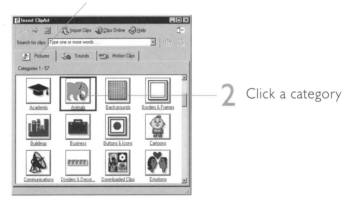

2 Click a category

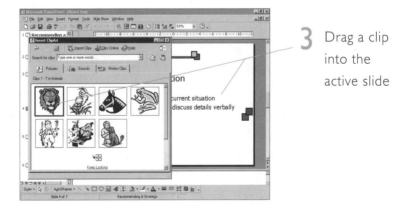

3 Drag a clip into the active slide

4 Release the mouse button – PowerPoint 2000 inserts the image

You can also download clips from the Web.
First ensure your Internet connection is live. Click this button:

in the Gallery. If this message appears:

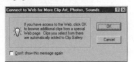

click OK. Your default browser now launches. Follow the on-screen instructions.

Providing the relevant slide has an associated AutoLayout which incorporates a clip art placeholder, you can use this to make inserting an image even easier.

Adding clip art via placeholders

In Normal or Notes Page view, go to the slide into which you want the clip art added. Carry out the following:

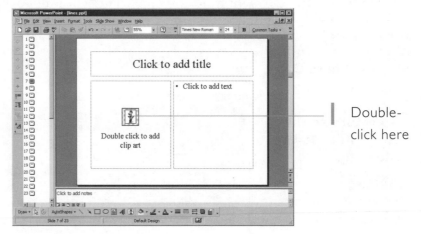

Double-click here

2 Follow step 2 on page 129

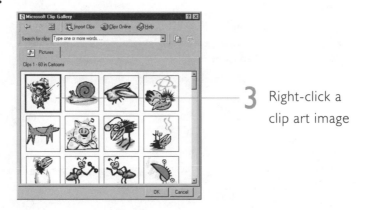

3 Right-click a clip art image

4 In the menu, click Insert

Working with the Clip Gallery

The clips in the Gallery have already had relevant categories applied to them...

By default, the Clip Gallery comes with numerous pre-defined categories e.g.

- Business

- Cartoons

- Communications

- Entertainment

- Photographs

- Seasons

- Special Occasions

To add a clip to the Gallery, click this button:

Use the Add clip to Clip Gallery dialog to locate and double-click the clip you want to add (first ensure the Files of type: field shows the correct format e.g. All Pictures). Complete the Clip Properties dialog, as appropriate, then click OK.

Applying categories to a clip

If the Clip Gallery isn't already open, pull down the Insert menu and do the following:

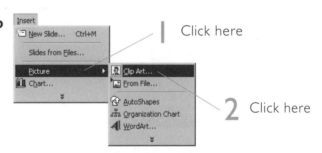

Click here

2 Click here

To remove a clip from the Gallery, right-click it. In the menu, click Delete. In the message which launches, click OK.

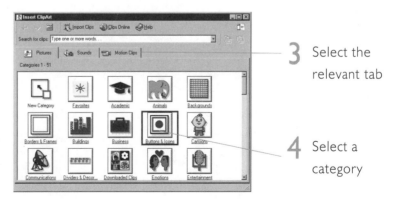

3 Select the relevant tab

4 Select a category

...cont'd

To close the Clip Gallery, click this button:

in the top right-hand corner.

5 Right-click a clip

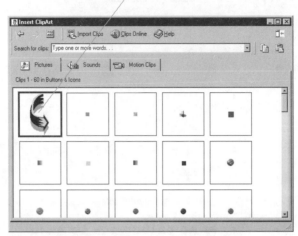

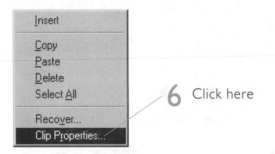

6 Click here

7 Activate this tab

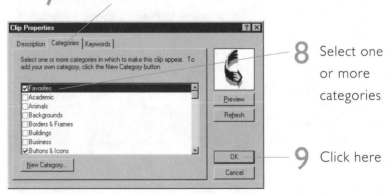

8 Select one or more categories

9 Click here

Creating new categories

To create a new category, do the following:

If the Gallery is already open, simply carry out steps 4-6.

1 If the Clip Gallery isn't currently open, pull down the Insert menu and carry out the following steps:

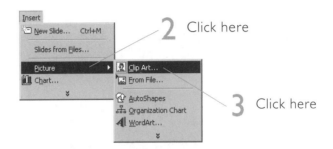

2 Click here

3 Click here

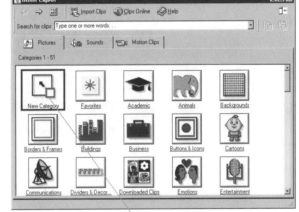

To apply the new category to clip art, carry out the relevant procedures on pages 131-132.

4 Click here

5 Name the new category

6 Click here

Renaming categories

If the Gallery is already open, simply carry out steps 4-8.

I If the Clip Gallery isn't currently open, pull down the Insert menu and carry out the following steps:

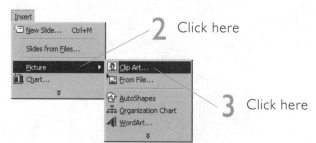

2 Click here

3 Click here

To delete a category, follow steps 1-3, as appropriate. Carry out steps 4-5. In step 6, select Delete Category. (Ignore steps 7-8.) In the message which launches, do the following:

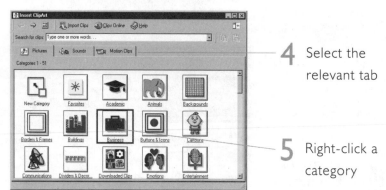

4 Select the relevant tab

5 Right-click a category

Click here

Open in New Window
Rename Category...
Delete Category
Paste Clips
Select All

Recover...

6 Click here

When you delete a category (see the above tip), the associated clips are not deleted.

7 Type in a new name

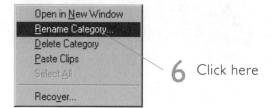

8 Click here

Using keywords

Clips in the Clip Gallery can (and do) have keywords associated with them (this means, for instance, that if you want to find a specific picture you can run a keyword search – see page 136). You can add additional keywords to any clip.

Adding keywords to a clip

Do the following:

If the Gallery is already open, simply carry out steps 2-7.

1 If the Clip Gallery isn't currently open, pull down the Insert menu and click Clip Art

2 Follow steps 3-6 on pages 131-132

3 Activate this tab

To delete a keyword, highlight it here:

Now click:

Remove Keyword

The keyword is removed immediately.

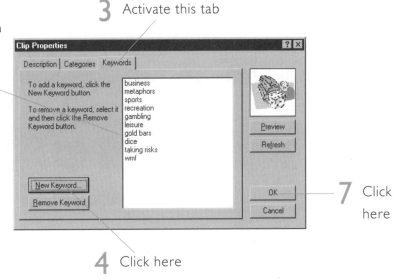

7 Click here

4 Click here

5 Type in the new keyword or keyword phrase

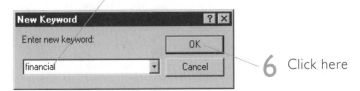

6 Click here

Searching for keywords

If the Gallery is already open, simply carry out steps 4-5.

To search for clips by one or more keywords, do the following:

I | If the Clip Gallery isn't currently open, pull down the Insert menu and carry out the following steps

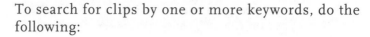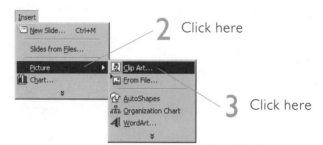

2 Click here

3 Click here

Moving the mouse pointer over a clip produces a box listing the first 3 associated keywords:

business,metaphors,people...
23.5 KB, wmf

4 Type in one or more keywords (or a key phrase), then press Enter

To see more Gallery clips, click this:

Keep Looking

after the final clip.

The end result:

5 Click the relevant tab (e.g. if you're looking for a sound clip, click Sounds)

Inserting pictures – an overview

Pictures PowerPoint 2000 can import into slides fall into two overall categories:

- bitmap images

- vector images

The following are brief details of each (note particularly that there is a certain level of crossover between the two formats):

Bitmap images

Bitmaps consist of pixels (dots) arranged in such a way that they form a graphic image. Because of the very nature of bitmaps, the question of 'resolution' – the sharpness of an image expressed in dpi (dots per inch) – is very important. Bitmaps look best if they're displayed at their correct resolution. You should bear this in mind if you're exporting files from other programs for inclusion in PowerPoint 2000 slides.

PowerPoint 2000 imports (i.e. translates into its own format) a wide variety of third-party bitmap formats.

See page 138 for details of specific bitmat and vector formats PowerPoint 2000 recognises.

Vector images

PowerPoint 2000 will also import vector graphics files in formats native to other programs. Vector images consist of, and are defined by, algebraic equations. One practical result of this is that they can be rescaled without any loss of definition. Another corollary is that they're less complex than bitmaps: they contain less detail.

Vector files can also include bitmap information. For example, PostScript files often have an illustrative header (used for preview purposes) which is a bitmap. This header is very often considerably inferior in quality when compared to the underlying picture.

Picture formats

Graphics formats PowerPoint 2000 will accept include the following (the column on the left shows the relevant file suffix):

Many bitmap formats have compression as an option. This allows bitmaps – often very large – to be stored on disk in much smaller files.

CGM	Computer Graphics Metafile. A vector format frequently used in the past, especially as a medium for clip-art transmission. Less often used nowadays.
EPS	Encapsulated PostScript. Perhaps the most widely used PostScript format. PostScript combines vector *and* bitmap data very successfully. Incorporates a low-resolution bitmap 'header' for preview purposes.
GIF	Graphics Interchange Format. A bitmap format developed for the on-line transmission of graphics data over the Internet. Just about any Windows program – and a lot more besides – will read GIF. Disadvantage: it can't handle more than 256 colours. Compression is supported.
PCD	(Kodak) PhotoCD. Used primarily to store photographs on CD.
PCX	An old stand-by. Originated with PC Paintbrush, a paint program. A bitmap format used for years to transfer graphics data between Windows applications.
TGA	Targa. A high-end bitmap format, and also a bridge with so-called low-end computers (e.g. Amiga and Atari). Often used in PC and Mac paint and ray-tracing programs because of its high-resolution colour fidelity.
TIFF	Tagged Image File Format. Suffix: TIF. A bitmap format and, if anything, even more widely used than PCX, across a whole range of platforms and applications.

Two further much-used formats are:

- **Windows Bitmap. A popular bitmap format. File suffix: BMP**
- **Windows Metafile. A frequently used vector format. Used for information exchange between just about all Windows programs. File suffix: WMF**

Inserting pictures

First, position the insertion point at the location within the active document where you want to insert the picture. Pull down the Insert menu and do the following:

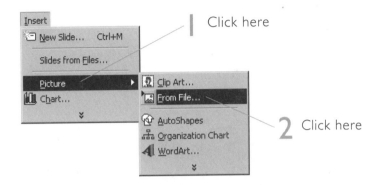

I Click here

2 Click here

4 Click here. In the drop-down list, click the drive that hosts the picture

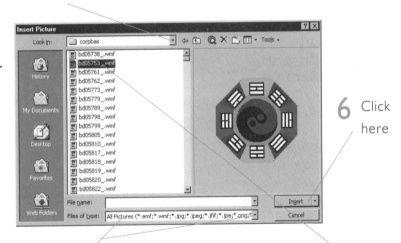

Re step 5 – you may have to double-click one or more folders first, to locate the picture file.

See the box on the right of the dialog for a preview of what the picture will look like when it's been imported.

6 Click here

3 Make sure All Pictures… is showing. If it isn't, click the arrow and select it from the drop-down list

5 Click a picture file

Working with clip art/pictures

You can't recolour imported bitmaps within PowerPoint 2000.

You can perform the following actions on clip art/pictures:

- resizing/cropping

- recolouring

- bordering

Resizing clip art/pictures

In Normal or Notes Pages view, select the clip art/picture. Now do the following:

Drag any handle inwards or outwards

If the Picture toolbar isn't currently on-screen, pull down the View menu and click Toolbars, Picture.

Cropping clip art/pictures

In Normal or Notes Pages view, select the clip art/picture. Now refer to the Picture toolbar and do the following:

Click here

You can also use the Picture toolbar to adjust image brightness and/or contrast.
   Select the image. Click this button in the toolbar:

   In the Format Picture dialog, activate the Picture tab. Drag the Brightness and Contrast sliders, as appropriate. Click OK.

2 Move the mouse pointer over any of the image handles and drag in to crop. Release the mouse button:

Before...

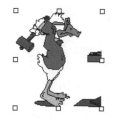

After

...cont'd

Recolouring clip art/pictures

In Normal or Notes Pages view, select the clip art/picture. Now refer to the Picture toolbar and do the following:

If the Picture toolbar isn't currently on-screen, pull down the View menu and click Toolbars, Picture.

| Click here

2 Click the colour you want to change

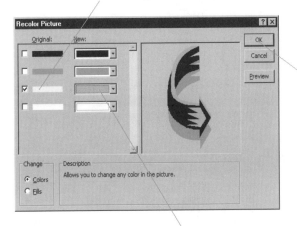

5 Click here

You can also animate clip art and pictures – see pages 165-167.

3 Click the box on the right

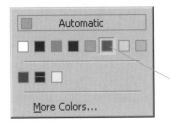

4 Select a new colour

...cont'd

By default, PowerPoint 2000 does not apply a border to inserted clip art/pictures. However, you can apply a wide selection of borders if you want. You can specify:

- the border style

- the border thickness

- the border colour

- whether the border is dashed

Applying a border

First, select the image you want to border. Then pull down the Format menu and click Picture. Now carry out step 1 below. Perform 2–3, as appropriate. Finally, carry out step 4:

To specify a border width, refer to the Weight field and do the following just before you carry out step 4:

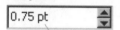

Type in a new width in points (1 inch = c. 72 points)

Re step 3 – if you want to apply a dotted (as opposed to a straight) border, click in the Dashed field instead and do the following:

Click here; click a style in the list

Ensure this tab is active

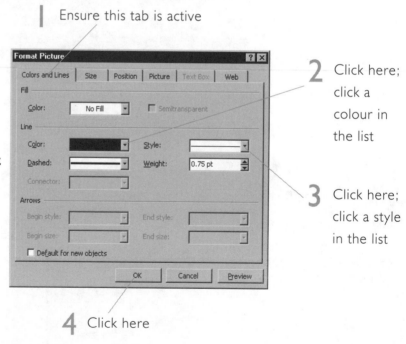

2 Click here; click a colour in the list

3 Click here; click a style in the list

4 Click here

Inserting sound clips

Sound clips can enhance slide impact tremendously.

Re step 1 – activate the category which hosts the clip before you right-click it.

Adding sound clips to slides

In Normal view, go to the slide into which you want to insert the sound clip. Now pull down the Insert menu and click Movies and Sounds, Sound from Gallery. Carry out the following steps:

To insert sound or movie clips into the Gallery, follow the procedures in the HOT TIP on page 131.

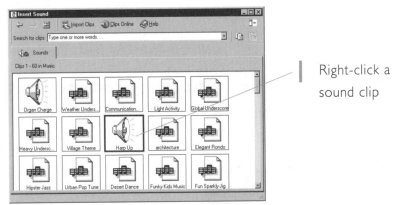

Right-click a sound clip

You must have a sound card installed in your PC to play back sound clips.

2 In the menu, click Insert

Playing a sound clip

In Normal view, go to the relevant slide. Now do the following:

You can also insert sound files into a slide.
  Pull down the Insert menu and click Movies and Sounds, Sound from File. In the Insert Sound dialog, locate and click a sound file. Finally, click OK.

Magnified view of sound icon

Double-click here

Inserting video clips

You can also insert video clips via the Clip Gallery.
Pull down the Insert menu and click Movies and Sounds, Movie from Gallery. In the Gallery, locate the movie clip you want to insert, then right-click it. In the menu, click Insert. In the message which launches, perform step 5 OR 6.

Video clips introduce a welcome note of animation into slides.

Adding video clips to slides

In Normal view, go to the slide into which you want to insert the video clip. Now pull down the Insert menu and click Movies and Sounds, Movie from File. Carry out the following steps:

2 Click here. In the drop-down list, click the drive that hosts the movie

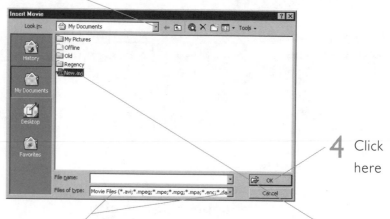

Re step 3 – you may have to double-click one or more folders first, to locate the movie file.

4 Click here

1 Make sure Movie Files… is showing. If it isn't, click the arrow and select it from the drop-down list

3 Click a movie file

To play a video clip within a slide, simply double-click it.

5 Click Yes to have the clip play automatically when you run your slide show

6 Click No if you want to play the clip manually (by clicking it).

Finalising slide shows

Use this chapter to fine-tune your presentation before you get ready to run it. You'll add summary slides, comments and speaker notes, and also create handouts, both within PowerPoint 2000 itself and also within Microsoft Word 2000 (because of its greater formatting capabilities). You'll apply the correct page setup parameters to your slide show; specify the correct printer setup; and then print out your slide show for proofing purposes. Finally, you'll export slides to third-party formats and edit presentations directly within Internet Explorer.

Covers

Chapter Seven

Fine-tuning your slide show

When you've finished developing your presentation (using the techniques discussed in earlier chapters), you should consider adding some last minute enhancements before you prepare it to be run. You can:

Summary slides list the main sections in your presentation for ease of access.

For how to create summary slides, see the DON'T FORGET tip on page 53. For how to insert hyperlinks (to make the summary slide even more useful), see Chapter 8.

- create summary slides (see the DON'T FORGET tip on the left

- insert internal comments

- add speaker notes

- create handouts

Internal comments aid the review/correction process by allowing presentations to be annotated by multiple users.

Speaker notes are a 'script' which you can create in Notes Page view (or in Notes view within Normal view) to help you give the presentation. Many PowerPoint 2000 users find these scripts very useful, even indispensable.

Handouts, on the other hand, are printed material which you supply to the slide show audience. Handouts consist of the following:

- an outline which the audience can follow as you speak

- copies of the individual slides (printed one or more to the page)

Additional preparations include:

- specifying page setup parameters

- specifying printer setup parameters

- printing out a proof copy of the presentation

- exporting slides to Word 2000 or other formats

Comments – an overview

If your presentation requires to be reviewed, you can insert the necessary comments into the relevant slides. When you've done this, other users can review your annotations, as appropriate. Alternatively, you can simply insert comments for your own information. For example, if you're not sure about the design of a particular slide but want to move on to the next, you could insert a comment (for your own attention) as a reminder that you need to go back to the original slide and review it later...

PowerPoint 2000 comments are self-formatting, self-wrapping text boxes:

Note:

Should we use 'Market Evaluation' rather than 'Market Summary' here?

Sample comment

When you create a comment, PowerPoint 2000 automatically inserts your name – in bold – at the start. (In the above example, this has been changed.) When you type in the comment text, the box wraps around the text.

Fine-tuning comments

When you've inserted comments, you can:

- resize them

- edit them

- view/hide them

- delete them if they've been actioned and are no longer required

- apply any formatting enhancements you want

Inserting a comment

In Normal view, go to the slide into which you want to insert the comment. Pull down the Insert menu and do the following:

 When you carry out step 1, all comments previously inserted into the current slide become visible.

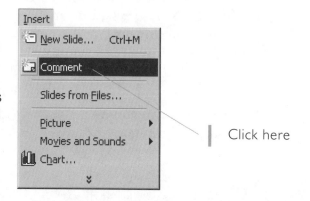

Click here

PowerPoint 2000 inserts a new comment, complete with your name as the author. Do the following:

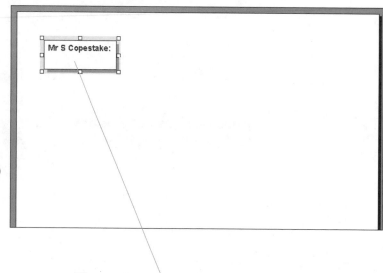

Mr S Copestake:

To resize a (completed) comment box, select it. Then use standard Windows resizing techniques.

2 Type in your comment, then click outside the comment box

Working with comments

If the **Reviewing toolbar isn't** currently on-screen, pull down the View menu and click Toolbars, Reviewing.

Viewing/hiding comments

To make comments visible or invisible (depending on the current setting), refer to the Reviewing toolbar and do the following:

Click here

To **reformat a comment, right-click** it. In the menu, click **Format Comment. Complete the Format Comment dialog as appropriate (e.g. to change the background colour, activate the Colors and Lines tab, then click a new colour in the Color box in the Fill section.)** Finally, click OK.

Note, however, that when you carry out step 1, the effects are global: all slides within the current slide show are affected.

Deleting comments

Ensure comments are currently visible (see above for how to do this). Then carry out the following steps:

Click anywhere on the comment frame

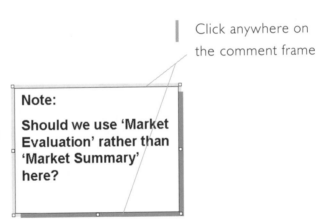

Note:

Should we use 'Market Evaluation' rather than 'Market Summary' here?

To **edit a comment, click in it, then make** the necessary **changes. When you've finished, click back in the slide itself.**

2 Press the Delete key

PowerPoint 2000 deletes the comment straightaway, without launching a warning message first.

Working with speaker notes

Every PowerPoint 2000 slide has a corresponding Notes page which displays:

- a reduced-size version of the slide

- a notes section complete with a notes placeholder

 If you have trouble working with note placeholders, try increasing the Zoom size.
Pull down the View menu and click Zoom. Click a higher zoom %. Click OK.

You can use the placeholder to enter notes which you'll refer to (either on-screen or from a printed copy) as you give your presentation.

You can create notes in the following ways:

- from within Notes Page view

- from within Normal view

Adding speaker notes within Notes Page view

If you're not already using Notes Page view, pull down the View menu and click Notes Page. Go to the slide into which you want to enter notes. Now do the following:

To print notes, carry out step 4 on page 158 (but select Notes Pages in the drop-down list).

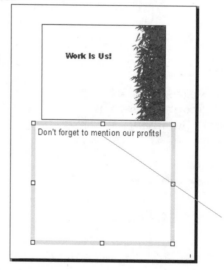

Work Is Us!

Don't forget to mention our profits!

Click in the placeholder. Type in your notes, then click outside the placeholder.

...cont'd

If you're already in Normal view, simply carry out steps 2-3.

If you want to add text or pictures to *all* notes pages, add them to the Notes master.
Pull down the View menu and click Master, Notes Master. Click in the note placeholder; add the relevant text and/or picture in the normal way. Finally, carry out the following:

Click here

To view note formatting accurately, click this button in the Standard toolbar (or fly-out):

Adding speaker notes within Normal view

If you're not already using Normal view, pull down the View menu and do the following.

Click here

2 Go to the slide into which you want to enter notes

Notes view

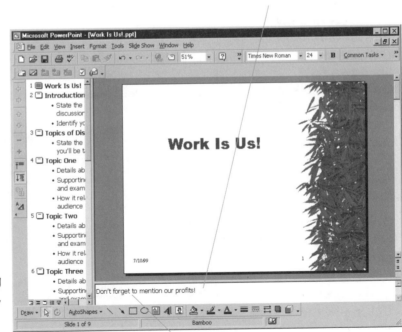

3 Type in the note text

Handouts

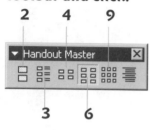

You can specify the number of slides per page. Refer to the Handout Master toolbar and click:

2   4   9

3   6

You create handouts with the help of the Handouts master.

Creating a handout

Pull down the View menu and do the following:

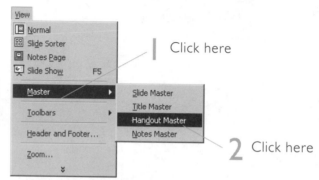

Click here

2 Click here

To print handouts, carry out step 4 on page 158 (but select Handouts in the drop-down list). Then complete the Handouts section.

PowerPoint 2000 now launches the Handouts master (with specific items – e.g. page numbers and footer text – already included):

Handout Master toolbar

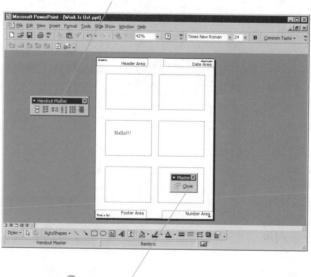

Before you carry out step 3, consider:

• **clicking in the Header area and replacing <header> with the relevant header text**

• **clicking in the Date area and replacing <date/ time> with a specific date/time**

3 Click here to close the Handout master

Exporting handouts to Word 2000

If the procedures listed on page 152 aren't adequate (for instance, if the presentation you're developing also involves a manual), you can create your handout in Word. When you do this, PowerPoint 2000 transfers all notes/slides automatically while letting you choose the handout format. You can then use the greater formatting capabilities innate in Word 2000 to produce the handout you need.

Exporting to Word 2000

Pull down the File menu and carry out the following steps:

For best results, click this button in the Standard toolbar (or its fly-out):

before carrying out steps 1-5.

1 Click here

2 Click here

If you want your slide show updated to take account of any editing changes you make in Word 2000 (see page 154), click here: before step 4.

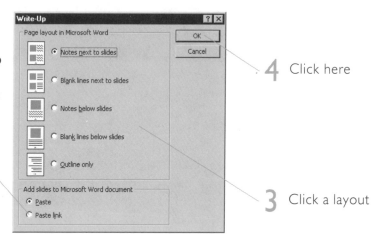

4 Click here

3 Click a layout

PowerPoint 2000 now starts Word (if it isn't already running) and:

- creates a new document

- inserts your presentation (with the requested layout) into the new document

Do the following:

 If you need help with using Word, consider buying a companion volume:

- **Word 97 in easy steps**
  or
- **Word 2000 in easy steps**

The inserted presentation

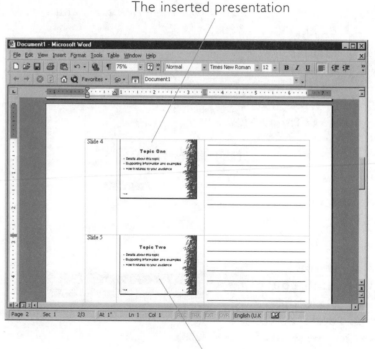

5 Edit the presentation in the normal way

If you clicked Paste link on page 153 (see the HOT TIP on the same page), any editing changes you make in Word are automatically reflected in your original presentation.

Page setup issues

Before you print a slide show, it's a good idea to specify:

- whether you want to print slides in Landscape (the default) or Portrait format

- the dimensions of the printed page

There are two aspects to every page size: a vertical measurement and a horizontal measurement. These can be varied according to orientation. There are two possible orientations:

Portrait   Landscape

Specifying page setup options

Pull down the File menu and click Page Setup. Now do the following:

Click here; select a slide size in the list

You can specify the start point from which slides are numbered.

Type in the start number here:

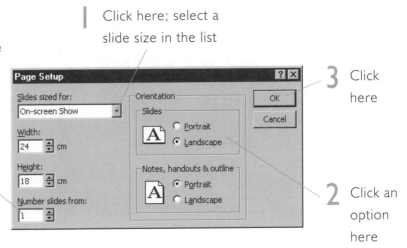

3 Click here

2 Click an option here

Printer setup

Before you can begin printing out your slide shows, you need to ensure that:

- the correct printer is selected (if you have more than one installed)

- the correct printer settings are in force

PowerPoint 2000 calls these collectively the 'printer setup'.

Irrespective of the printer selected, the settings vary in accordance with the job in hand. For example, most printer drivers (the software which 'drives' the printer) allow you to specify whether or not you want pictures printed. Additionally, they often allow you to specify the resolution or print quality of the output...

Selecting the printer and/or settings

At any time before you're ready to print a presentation, pull down the File menu and click Print. Now do the following:

Click here; select the printer you want from the list

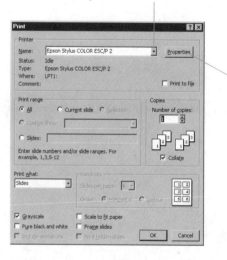

2 Click here to adjust printer settings (see your printer's manual for how to do this)

Now complete the remainder of the Print dialog, prior to printing your slide show (see pages 157–158).

Printing – an overview

You can print any presentation component. These include:

- slides

- notes

- outlines

- handouts

- comments

To print internal comments, simply ensure that they're currently visible. (See page 149 for how to do this.)

You can also:

- specify the number of copies

- specify slide ranges (e.g. slides 1-6 inclusive and 11)

- have printed copies collated

- print out slides in greyscale, or black-and-white ('mono')

- proportionately scale printed output up or down to match your paper size

Alternatively, you can simply opt to print your presentation with the default options in force (PowerPoint 2000 provides a 'fast-track' approach to this).

Collation

Collation is the process whereby PowerPoint 2000 prints one full copy of a presentation at a time. For instance, if you're printing three copies of an 8-slide presentation, PowerPoint 2000 prints slides 1-8 of the first slide show, followed by slides 1-8 of the second and slides 1-8 of the third.

Collation is only possible if you're printing multiple copies of a slide show.

Printing your slide show

Ensure Collate is selected if you want output collated.

Click Scale to fit paper to have output scaled evenly to fit your paper size.

Ensure Grayscale is selected if you want to print out in greyscale. Click Pure black & white to print out in mono.

Re step 3 – separate non-adjacent slides with commas – e.g. to print slides 5, 12 & 16 type in: '5,12,16'. Enter contiguous slides with dashes – e.g. to print slides 12 to 23 inclusive, type: '12-23'. (Omit the quote marks in all examples.)

Printing a presentation

First carry out steps 1-2 on page 156. Pull down the File menu and click Print. Now carry out any of steps 1-5 below, as appropriate. Finally, follow step 6.

1 Click here to print only the active slide

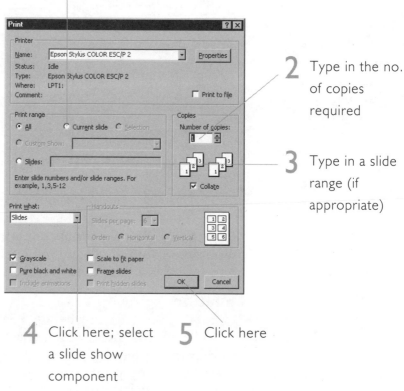

2 Type in the no. of copies required

3 Type in a slide range (if appropriate)

4 Click here; select a slide show component

5 Click here

Fast-track printing

To print using all the default settings, without launching the Print dialog, simply click the Print button on the Standard toolbar:

Exporting slide shows/slides

See pages 137-138 for broad details of bitmap and vector graphics formats.

After step 1, double-click one or more folders until you reach the one you want to export your slide show to.

Re step 2 – if you select a graphics format (e.g. GIF), each slide is saved as a separate picture file.

After step 4, complete the message which launches, if appropriate (click Yes to export all slides, or No to export only the active one).

It's sometimes useful to be able to export entire presentations or individual slides to third-party formats. For example, you may want to export the whole of a slide show to:

• an earlier version of PowerPoint 2000, so you can work with it on a different machine

• a RTF outline, which allows your presentation to be read by many different software programs

Alternatively, you may wish to export one slide (or all slides within a presentation) as a picture, for example in GIF format.

Exporting slides

Pull down the File menu and click Save As. Carry out the following steps:

1 Click here. In the drop-down list, click the drive you want to host the exported file

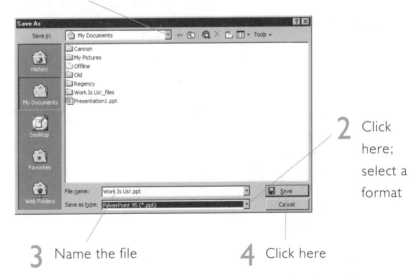

2 Click here; select a format

3 Name the file

4 Click here

Editing in Internet Explorer

Using the technique discussed here, PowerPoint 2000 files, converted to HTML format and saved to the Web, can be run by the majority of Internet users.

When you create HTML files from within PowerPoint 2000 (see below), they can be edited from within Internet Explorer 5.

Look at the illustration below:

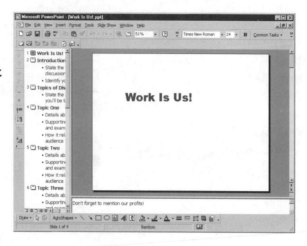

When you've created slide notes, PowerPoint automatically creates special note frames during conversion to HTML format.

This is a slide show produced with the AutoContent wizard. You can use the techniques discussed on page 64 to convert it to a HTML file. Once the HTML file has been opened in Internet Explorer, do the following:

After step 1, the file is opened within PowerPoint 2000, with the formatting intact despite the 'round-trip'.
  Use standard editing techniques to make the relevant amendments.

Click here

Preparing slide shows

Use this chapter to prepare your presentation to be run. This involves applying transitions (the process of determining how adjacent slides supersede each other); animations (special effects applied to individual slide objects); and hyperlinks (buttons which jump to specific slides or locations). You'll also stipulate the length of time each slide is on-screen. Finally, you'll create a custom slide show (for a specific audience) and ensure your presentation is set up correctly.

Covers

Chapter Eight

Preparation – an overview

See Chapter 9 for how to perform – 'run' – slide shows.

PowerPoint 2000 provides a wide assortment of techniques you can use to ensure that your presentation has the maximum impact. These are all ways of preparing your slide show for its eventual performance.

You can:

- specify transitions (interactions between individual slides)

- apply animations (used to control how each slide element is introduced to the audience)

- insert hyperlinks (buttons which – when clicked – jump to additional slides)

- customise slide timings (the intervals between individual slides)

- customise the presentations setup

Presentation setup

Presentation setup specifies:

- which slides do or do not display (via custom slide shows). Use this to prepare presentations which are tailored for specific audiences (some slides may not be suitable for a given recipient)

- the type of slide show delivery. You can determine whether presentations run:

  — normally (i.e. orchestrated by the presenter)

  — in a special window

  — at a conference kiosk

- whether the presentation runs in 'loop' mode

- whether slides are advanced manually, or using the preset timings

Transitions

Transitions add visual interest to presentations by customising the crossover between individual slides. PowerPoint 2000 provides numerous separate transition effects. These include:

Random Transition	PowerPoint 2000 selects and applies the transition
Blinds Horizontal or Vertical	The next slide displays like a blind
Checkerboard Across or Down	The next slide displays with a chequered pattern
Box In or Out	The next slide displays as an increasing or decreasing box

When you apply a transition to a specific slide, the effect takes place between the previous and selected slides.

You can specify transitions' effects:

*   on all slides within a presentation

*   on individual slides

Applying transitions to the whole of a slide show

In any view, pull down the Slide Show menu and do the following:

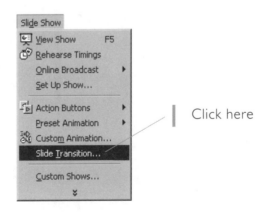

Click here

...cont'd

Now carry out the following steps:

To apply a sound with the transition, **click here:** In the list, click a sound. Then carry out step 4.

2 Click here

4 Click here

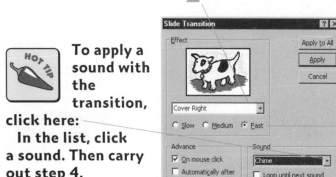

3 Click a transition speed

If you're not currently in Slide Sorter view, pull down the View menu and click Slide Sorter.

Applying transitions to specific slides

In Slide Sorter view, do the following:

2 Click here

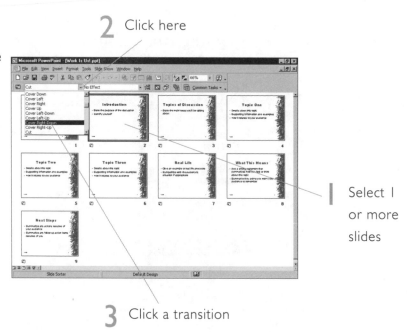

Re step 1 – to select more than one slide, hold down Ctrl as you click the slide icons.

Select 1 or more slides

3 Click a transition

Animations

You can use animations to:

- introduce objects onto a slide one at a time (by default, they all appear on-screen at once)

- apply special effects to objects

Having objects appear in a staggered way maximises slide impact; the eye is drawn to areas of specific interest in a way which makes them more prominent.

Imposing special effects on objects is particularly useful in the following scenarios:

- having individual items in a bulleted list appear one at a time

- having pictures, clip art or charts become prominent slowly

You can apply preset animations or create your own.

 You can also apply animations to an entire slide. In Slide Sorter view, select one or more slides. Then follow steps 1-2.

Applying a preset animation

In Normal view, pull down the Slide Show menu and do the following:

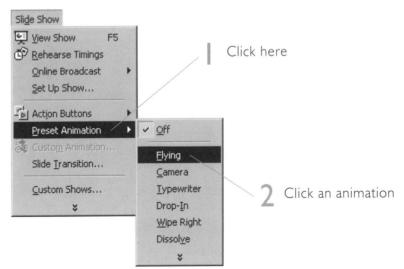

Click here

2 Click an animation

...cont'd

 If you create more than one animation, also click the Order & Timing tab and specify the animation sequence. To do this, select an animation in the Animation order: field and click:

or

Repeat as often as necessary. Finally, perform step 6.

 Perform steps 2-5 as often as necessary. Finally, carry out step 6.

 Re step 4 – with some animations, select the direction of movement; with others, choose the speed.

Customising animations

In Normal view, right-click the object you want to animate and do the following:

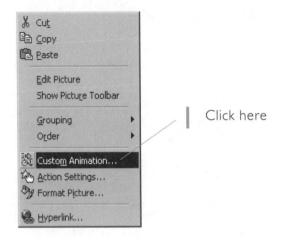

Click here

2 Select the object you want to animate – ensure a ✔ appears

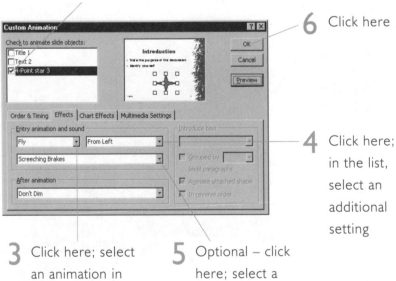

6 Click here

4 Click here; in the list, select an additional setting

3 Click here; select an animation in the list

5 Optional – click here; select a sound in the list

...cont'd

Previewing animations

In Normal view, select the object you want to preview. Pull down the Slide Show menu and do the following:

Previewing also plays any associated sound tracks.

Click here

When the Animation Preview window launches, it automatically previews the selected object/ animation. If you want to repeat this, simply click anywhere within the window.

PowerPoint 2000 now launches the Animation Preview window:

Animation Preview window

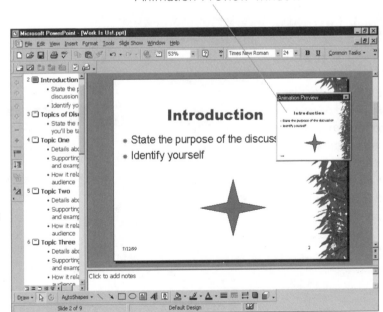

To close the Animation Preview window, click here:

in the upper-right corner.

Inserting hyperlinks

You can insert hyperlinks into slides. In PowerPoint 2000, hyperlinks are 'action buttons' which you can click (while a presentation is being run) to jump to a prearranged destination immediately. This can be:

'URL' stands for Uniform Resource Locator. URLs are unique addresses for World Wide Web sites.

(If you need more information on the Internet, see 'Internet UK in easy steps').

• preset slide targets (for instance, the first, last, next or previous slide)

• a specific slide (where *you* select a slide from a special dialog)

• a URL (providing you have a live Internet connection)

• another PowerPoint presentation

• another file

Inserting an action button

In Normal or Notes Page view, pull down the Slide Show menu. Do the following:

Action buttons are actually AutoShapes. See pages 99-106 for how to work with AutoShapes.

In particular, carry out the procedures in the HOT TIP on page 99 to add text which describes the destination (e.g. 'Slide 13').

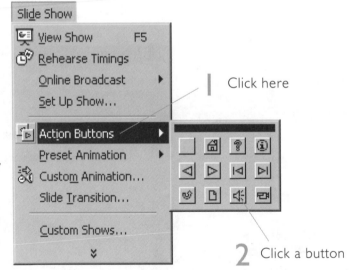

Click here

2 Click a button

...cont'd

Now position the mouse pointer at the location on the slide where you want the button inserted. Hold down the left mouse button and drag to define the button. Release the mouse button and carry out the following steps:

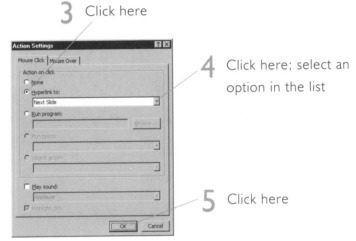

3 Click here

4 Click here; select an option in the list

5 Click here

Re. step 4 – complete any further dialog which launches. Click OK, then follow step 5.

The illustration below shows an inserted action button/hyperlink:

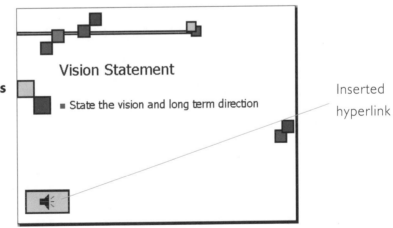

Vision Statement

■ State the vision and long term direction

Inserted hyperlink

Hyperlinks only become active when you run your slide show.

Specifying slide timing

The rehearsal method (a kind of dummy-run) is especially suitable for ensuring that the slide timings you insert are workable.

You can specify how long each slide is on-screen, and by implication the duration of the entire presentation. There are two ways to do this:

• from within Slide Sorter view (either singly, or for every slide)

• by 'rehearsing' the presentation

Applying timings in Slide Sorter view

Select one or more slides, then pull down the Slide Show menu and do the following:

Click here

You can follow the procedures here to amend *existing* timings (or to reset them to zero, if appropriate).

Re step 3 – click Apply to All to have the timing applied to *every* slide in the show.

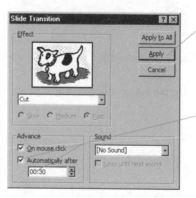

3 Click here to apply the new timings to the selected slide(s)

2 Click here, then type in a slide duration in seconds

...cont'd

Rehearsing slides uses a special PowerPoint 2000 feature: the Slide Meter.

Applying timings with the Slide Meter

In any view, pull down the Slide Show menu and do the following:

| Click here

PowerPoint launches its rehearsal window, with the first slide (and the Slide Meter) displayed. Do the following:

2 This timer counts the interval until the next slide; when the timing is right, follow step 3

The Slide Meter

3 Click here

After step 3, PowerPoint 2000 moves to the next slide. Repeat steps 2 and 3 until all the slides have had intervals allocated. Finally, a message appears. Do the following:

4 Click here

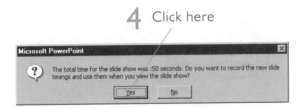

Creating custom slide shows

PowerPoint 2000 lets you create custom slide shows.
Custom shows allow you to adopt a mix-and-match
approach by selecting specific slides from the active
presentation. This allows you to tailor a base slide show for
specific audiences and/or occasions.

Creating a custom show

Open the relevant slide show. Select one or more slides,
then pull down the Slide Sorter menu and do the following:

**For how to
run a
custom
show, see
Chapter 9.**

Click here

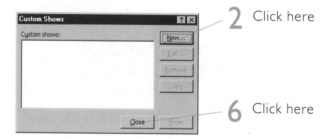

2 Click here

6 Click here

3 Name the custom show

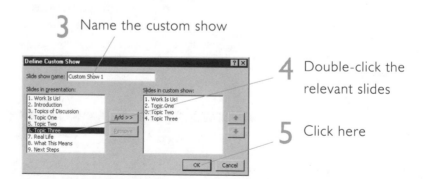

4 Double-click the
relevant slides

5 Click here

...cont'd

Once you've set up a custom slide show, you can:

- remove slides

- add new slides

- move slides up or down

Editing a custom show

Follow step 1 on page 172. Then carry out steps 2-3 below. To remove a slide, perform steps 4 and 5. To change the slide order, follow step 4, and then 6 OR 7. Finally, carry out step 8.

2 Click a custom show

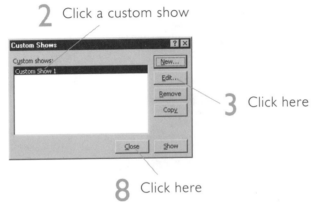

3 Click here

8 Click here

 To add a new slide to the custom show, double-click it here:

4 Click a slide

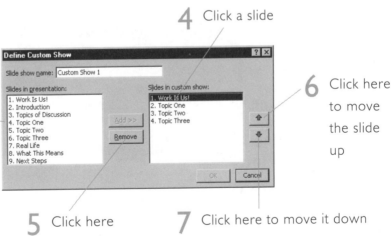

6 Click here to move the slide up

5 Click here

7 Click here to move it down

Final preparations

The definitive stage in slide show preparation involves telling PowerPoint 2000:

- the type of presentation you want to run

- whether you want it to run perpetually

- whether you want each slide to appear automatically

Setting up a presentation

Pull down the Slide Show menu and carry out step 1 below. Then carry out step 2 and/or 3. Finally, perform step 4.

Click here

For a looped slide show, select Loop continuously until 'Esc' before carrying out step 4.

2 Click a slide show type

Re step 3 – choose Manually if you want to control slide transition, or 'Using timings, if present' if you want transition to be in line with the timings you set on pages 170-171.

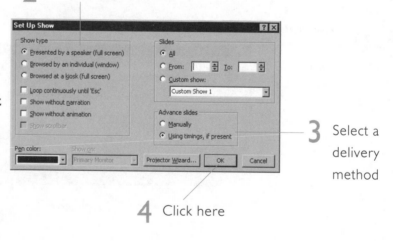

3 Select a delivery method

4 Click here

Presenting slide shows

Use this chapter to learn how to present your slide show to a live audience. You'll discover how to move around in live presentations, and how to accentuate slide areas with the Light Pen. Next you'll save your slide show as a 'run-time' file (so it can be run on machines which don't have PowerPoint 2000 installed). Finally, you'll broadcast your slide show over intranets, then get information, tips and software downloads directly from the Web.

Covers

Chapter Nine

Running your presentation

By now, your presentation is ready to run. PowerPoint 2000 lets you:

1. present it to a live audience (this is the most common scenario)

2. create a special run-time file (which enables slide shows to be run on PCs which don't have PowerPoint 2000 installed)

3. publish your slide show on the World Wide Web, using Microsoft's enhanced HTML format (see page 63 for more information). This means that anyone with Internet Explorer 4 or above can run it in a way which – since the original formatting is preserved with high fidelity – is more or less identical to 1. above

Running standard slide shows live

Pull down the Slide Show menu and do the following:

To start a broadcast, pull down the Slide Show menu and click Online Broadcast, Begin Broadcast. Click Start.

Click here

For help with any aspect of slide show broadcasting, see your system administrator.

Carry out the additional step on the facing page.

...cont'd

If you allocated slide timings (using one of the techniques on pages 170-171) AND selected 'Using timings, if present' (in step 3 on page 174), PowerPoint 2000 displays the next slide automatically.

If, on the other hand, you selected Manually in step 3 on page 174, follow step 2 on the immediate right. Repeat as and when necessary.

(For details of other navigational techniques, see page 178.)

To terminate a slide show before the end, press Esc.

PowerPoint 2000 launches the first slide in a special window:

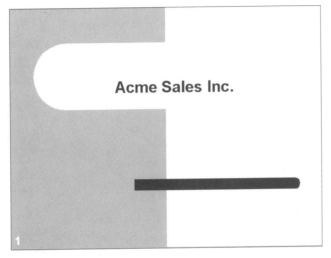

Acme Sales Inc.

2 Left-click once to view the next slide – but see the DON'T FORGET tip

Running custom slide shows live

Pull down the Slide Show menu and click Custom Show. Now do the following:

Select a custom show

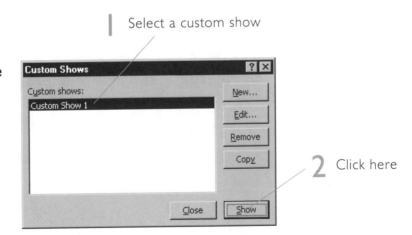

2 Click here

Navigating through slide shows

Re the black/ white screen commands, repeat the appropriate keystroke to return to the normal screen.

Re the 'specified slide' method – to go to slide 6 (for example), type '6' (without the quotes) then press Enter.

**For instance, you can use the menu to go to a slide with a given title – click Go, By Title then select a title in the sub-menu...
(See also the facing page.)**

Navigating – the keystroke approach

When you run a presentation, you're actually using a special view called Slide Show. There are special commands you can use to move around in Slide Show view. Press any of the keystrokes listed in the left column to produce the desired result (shown on the right):

Enter; Page Down; or the Spacebar	jumps to the next slide
Page Up or Backspace	jumps to the previous slide
B or full stop	launches a black screen
W or comma	launches a white screen
'Slide number' plus Enter	goes to the specified slide (see the DON'T FORGET tip)
S	stops/restarts an automatic slide show (i.e. one where the presenter is not initiating slide progression manually)
Home	jumps to the first slide
End	jumps to the last slide
Esc	ends a slide show

Navigating – the mouse approach

You can also use mouse actions:

Single left-click	jumps to the next slide
Hold down left and right button for 2 seconds	jumps to the first slide
Single right-click	produces a helpful menu

...cont'd

Navigating with the Slide Navigator

You can also use a dialog route to navigate in Slide Show view.

Within Slide Show view, right-click once. In the menu which appears, do the following:

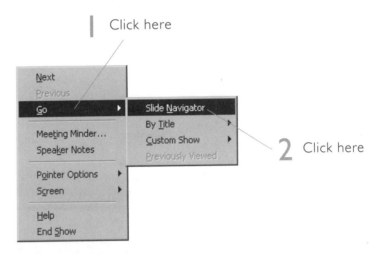

Click here

If you want to run a custom slide show, follow step 1. Ignore steps 2-3 – instead, click Custom Show. In the sub-menu, select the name of the custom show.

2 Click here

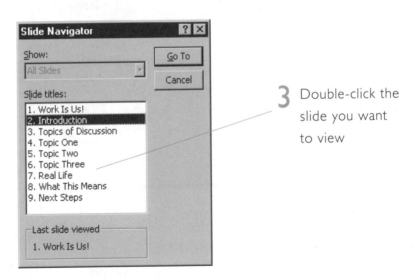

3 Double-click the slide you want to view

Emphasising slide shows

PowerPoint 2000 lets you emphasise slides during a live presentation. You do this by using a feature known as the Light Pen.

Using the Light Pen
In Slide Show view, right-click once. Do the following:

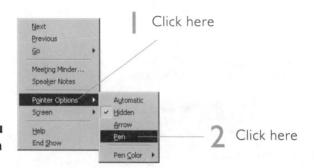

Click here

Click here

Marks you make with the Light Pen are only temporary: they disappear when you move to another slide.

You can specify the colour used by the Light Pen. Right-click the slide. In the menu, click Pointer Options, Pen Color. In the sub-menu, click a colour.

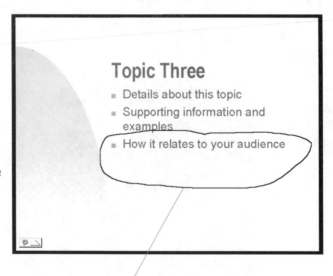

3 Place the mouse pointer (it changes to a pen) near the area you want to emphasise, then drag to accentuate it

Run-time presentations

If you need to take a slide show to an audience, you can have PowerPoint 2000 create a compressed – 'run-time' – file (occupying more than one floppy disk, if necessary) containing:

- the active presentation

- ancillary information (e.g. typeface details)

- a minimal PowerPoint 2000 viewer (a small program which enables PCs which lack PowerPoint 2000 to run presentations)

 **Run-time files don't have to contain typeface data or the PowerPoint 2000 viewer: these are optional, though often desirable.**

PowerPoint 2000 uses a special wizard to create run-time files.

Using the Pack and Go Wizard
In any view, pull down the File menu and click Pack and Go. Carry out the following steps:

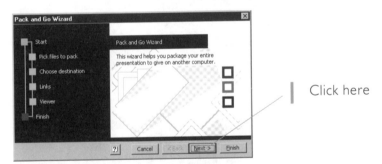

Click here

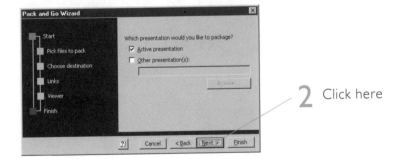

2 Click here

...cont'd

Re step 5 – select Embed TrueType Fonts if your slide show uses typefaces which are unlikely to be on the destination PC. This results in a bigger file, but one which is guaranteed to run correctly.

Now perform the following additional steps:

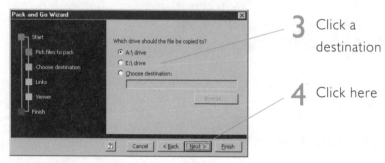

3 Click a destination

4 Click here

To unload your run-time file on the destination PC, launch Explorer. Go to the folder containing the file. Activate PNGSETUP.EXE. Follow the on-screen instructions.

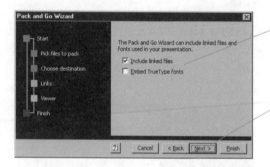

5 Select any (or both) of these

6 Click here

To view the slide show, start Explorer. In the folder which holds your slide show, activate PPVIEW32.EXE (the viewer). Double-click the show in the Look in: field.

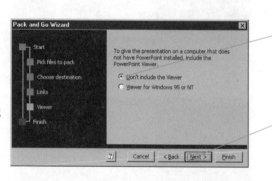

7 Ensure this is selected to include the viewer

8 Click here

9 In the final wizard dialog, click this button:

Assistance on the Web

 To access the Tips and Tricks site, follow steps 1-2. Now click Tips & Tricks for PowerPoint 2000. Click a tip e.g.
<u>Frequently Asked Questions</u>
Follow the on-screen instructions.

 To access the Technical Support site, follow steps 1-2. Now click Microsoft Technical Support for PowerPoint. In the screen which launches, click a topic e.g.
<u>Troubleshooter for PowerPoint</u>
Follow the on-screen instructions.

 To access a newsgroup, follow steps 1-2. Now click PowerPoint Newsgroups. Click a newsgroup e.g.
<u>Office Setup</u>
Follow the on-screen instructions.

PowerPoint 2000 has inbuilt links to dedicated Microsoft World Wide Web pages. Provided you have:

- a modem

- a live connection to an Internet service provider

you can connect almost immediately to:

- helpful articles which are specific to PowerPoint 2000-related questions and topics

- Microsoft technical support for PowerPoint 2000

- Access to dedicated PowerPoint 2000 newsgroups

- a special Tips and Tricks site which provides useful insights into ways in which you can improve your use of PowerPoint 2000

- a special site from which you can download software updates which are both useful and free

Launching the PowerPoint 2000 Web site

With a live Internet connection, pull down the Help menu and do the following:

Click here

After step 2, a further screen launches. Do one of the following:

- **click Articles for Microsoft PowerPoint 2000, then click an article**

or

- **follow any of the procedures in the tips on page 183**

You can also access a special Web page which lets you download useful software updates. In step 2, click Downloads. Now do the following:

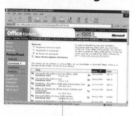

Click a topic

Read the on-screen instructions. When you're ready to download, click:

Download Now!

The PowerPoint 2000 Welcome page launches. Carry out step 2 or 3:

2 Click Assistance for helpful articles

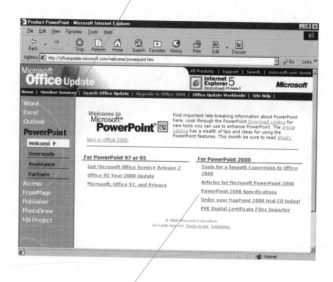

3 Click any article here

The end result:

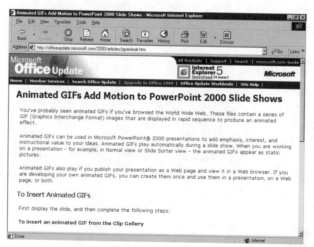

One of the many available articles

Running presentations in Explorer

One corollary of Microsoft's elevation of the HTML format to a status which rivals that of its own formats (see page 63) is that:

A.   presentations display authentically in Internet Explorer (especially if you're using version 4 or above)

B.   you can even run presentations from within Internet Explorer

Running slide shows in Internet Explorer

First, use the techniques discussed on pages 63-64 to convert an existing presentation to HTML format. Open this in Internet Explorer. Now do the following:

B. means that slide shows converted to HTML format and saved to the Web can be run by the majority of Internet users.

Click here to run your show in Full-Screen mode

Here, the slide show is being displayed in Internet Explorer 5.

You can hide the slide outline, if you want. Simply click here:

Internet Explorer now launches the first slide of your presentation so that it occupies the whole screen:

To halt the slide show before the end, press

Esc.

If you allocated slide timings (using one of the techniques on pages 170-171) AND selected 'Using timings, if present' in step 3 on page 174, Internet Explorer progresses to the next slide when the relevant interval has elapsed. If, on the other hand, you selected Manually in step 3 on page 174, left-click once when you want to move on to the next slide. And so on to the end...

To close Internet Explorer, press

Alt+F4.

When the last slide has been displayed, a special screen displays with the following text:

End of slide show, click to exit.

Click anywhere to return to Internet Explorer's main screen.

Index